Bearstone Blackie, Detective

Ray Pace

Cover Illustration of Bearstone Blackie by Julia Pace

"The gypsies believe the bear to be a brother to man because he has the same body beneath his hide, because he drinks beer, because he enjoys music and because he likes to dance."

Ernest Hemingway

"There's what we expect bears to do and then there's what they do. Sometimes the two don't match."

Joe Clark, Research Ecologist, University of Tennessee.

This book is dedicated to the Fox and the Bruin, and the wonderful writers who hang out in Waimea and Kohala.

This is a work of fiction. Any resemblance to truth may be found in the mind of the reader.

Table of Contents

Bearstone Blackie, an Introduction
By Ray Pace

Summer, 2016 in Waimea on the Big Island of Hawaii was a special time. Writers were holding a series of sessions at the Holo Holo Ku clubhouse, next to the Paniolo Heritage Center, a place honoring cowboys, horses, and cattle. Waimea is noted for its ranch style living and increasingly for the talented writers who come from all over the island to meet.

The sessions featured works in progress from poets, novelists, short story writers, and journalists. Also featured were potluck luncheons that left no one hungry.

I had just finished the first draft of a novel that dealt with a freelance detective in Las Vegas. I was having fun wrapping up the final chapter and receiving cheers from the gathered writers as I finished reading it. The wonderful glow lasted about a minute. Then came the nagging thought. What do I do next?

Editing the Vegas novel would have been a logical choice, but I didn't want to lose my edge. I wanted to keep writing something.

I shouldn't have worried.

I caught a glimpse of him when I looked up.

It was Bearstone, standing near the buffet and smiling at me.

I knew what he was thinking.

"If that guy Nick can do all those things and make wry comments in that Vegas book, why can't a bear be the leading character in your next book?"

Later we talked it over.

"I'm not trying to say anything bad about them," Bearstone said, "But if a couple of schlemiels like my cousins Winnie and Paddington can make it by screwing things up, think what a bear detective could do."

"Bear detective?" I asked.

"Sure," he said. "What did you think, I was going to stand in the park selling balloons to three-year-olds? What kind of smarmy pap would that be?"

I shrugged.

"See, that's what's wrong with people, especially when it comes to storybook characters," he said. "They take all that Mother Goose and Brothers Grimm stuff and they treat it like it's gospel, like that's the way it all went down. They won't even do that for the New York Times."

"And somehow, you know differently?" I asked.

"Believe me, I'd look into that stuff and get the real info," he said. "A lot of these so-called kids' stories need an adult's oversight."

He nonchalantly took a croissant out of a bag from the Hungry Bear Donut Factory and took a bite. He offered a croissant to me. It was a delicious buttery bribe.

"Bearstone Blackie, detective," he said. "I represent the Bear With Us Detective Agency in El Bruno."

"And where pray tell, is El Bruno?" I asked.

"I'm surprised," he said. "You're the talented writer. I'm sure you can come up with a reasonable location."

"I take it that's where the Hungry Bear Donut Factory should be?" I asked.

"Love it if it were," he said. "Ultimately, it will be between the ears of the reader. No matter how much you go to lengths describing it, everyone's image of the place will be different."

I nodded.

"You mean it will be like a cartoon in the mind?" I asked.

He nodded and took another bite of a croissant.

"If it's excellent, it might be a Rembrandt in mind," he said. "It all depends on how good a writer you turn out to be."

"And you?" I asked.

"I'll be there to give you good advice," he said. "But, that's not my primary role. I'm the handsome leading man who tosses out snappy rejoinders and solves cases."

"Anything else I need to know, should we go ahead with this venture?" I asked.

He thought for a moment.

"I should have a knock-out babe for a girlfriend," he said. "How does the name Beartina sound to you?"

The Mysterious Caper at Bear Manor

The phone rang on my desk at the Bear With Us Detective Agency. I answered it on the first ring. There was a gruff voice on the other end.

"I'm looking for Detective Bearstone Blackie. This is Papa Bear from Bear Manor in El Bruno."

"You found him," I said. "What can I do for you?"

"Mysterious happenings in our house. Many detectives come out to take a look, but nothing gets better. It's always the same problem. Can you get out later today and take a look? They say you're the best in the business."

I wrote down the address and told him I'd be there.

It was a beautiful log house with matching beehives at each end of the property.

I knocked on the front door.

A moment later a blonde girl answered.

"Can I help you?"

"I'm Bearstone Blackie, private detective. I'm looking for Papa Bear. We have an appointment."

"I'm Goldie," she said. "I'm afraid they've done it again."

"What have they done?" I asked.

"They've gone off on a walk in the woods and forgotten about your appointment."

"Maybe they're on their way back," I said. "I can wait."

"Come in," she said. "I can probably explain what's been happening."

She led the way to the kitchen. On the countertop next to the sink were three bowls.

"They make their own porridge," she said. "They make it too hot to eat, and so they decide to take a walk while it cools off. Problem is that when they get back, they always say that there's something wrong with what they made."

"Something wrong?" I asked.

"Go ahead, taste them," she said. "It won't matter."

I tried the biggest bowl, Papa Bear's. It was way too hot, and when I tried to get the spoon out, it got stuck. The whole thing set up like it was concrete or plaster of Paris.

I tried the smallest bowl, Baby Bear's. It was cold and flavorless. With one slurp, I drank the whole thing down.

"Not much of a porridge," I said to Goldie

"Never is," she said.

The middle-sized bowl was just right with good flavor and the right temperature.

"That's Mama Bear's bowl," Goldie said. "She knows her porridge."

I finished what was left of Mama Bear's porridge and asked what was next.

She led me into the living room.

"Furniture is a big problem for them," she said. "They just had these three chairs delivered to replace the ones they had, which were just like these."

"What happened?" I asked.

"They get the chairs made-to-order," she said. "Papa Bear's chair is full of sharp angles and doesn't let the sitter sit into it. It's like sitting on plastic covered concrete. Try it out."

5

I sat down, and she was right. If a chair ever needed fixing, this was the one. Luckily there was a fireplace poker nearby, and I was able to modify the cushions.

"Baby Bear's chair is over here," she said. "It looks good, but it's cheaply made."

She wasn't kidding there. The minute I sat down on it, it fell into a dozen pieces.

"Are you okay?" She asked.

"Okay enough," I said struggling to my feet. "What's with the chair in the middle?"

"That's Mama Bear's. She gets cold a lot, so the chair is always heated for her."

I sat down in it and immediately started sweating like I was in a steam bath. Puddles of sweat formed on every surface of the chair before I could squeeze my way out of it.

Next, she showed me the newly-delivered beds. Papa Bear's waterbed had too little water in it. It was easy to fix. I fastened a hose to it and turned it on full blast. I looked over at Baby Bear's waterbed. It had a nice rounded top on it. I thought it would be comfortable, but when I tried to get on it, the whole thing burst water all over the room.

Mama Bear's waterbed seemed just right, but then I realized her heater was on 'very hot, ' and I started sweating again.

"Don't worry," Goldie said. "This stuff happens all the time."

Just then we heard sounds from the kitchen. The Bear family was back.

"Someone's been fooling with my porridge." Papa Bear said. "My favorite spoon is stuck in concrete."

"Someone's been fooling with my porridge," said Mama Bear. "It's all gone."

"Mine, too," said Baby Bear.

They went to the living room.

"Someone's been beating up my new chair," Papa Bear said.

"Someone's been sweating all over my new chair," Mama Bear said.

"Someone's destroyed my new chair," Baby Bear said.

"Well, it's a good thing I'm here," I said, entering the room.

"Who are you?" They all asked.

"I'm Bearstone Blackie, the private detective you hired," I said. "You have a problem with your waterbeds, too. One of them has burst, and another may be getting ready to boil. The other is filling up from the hose because I suspect it has a leak."

Goldie raced back to the bedroom to turn off the water.

"What caused all this destruction?" Papa Bear wanted to know.

"Why does this keep happening?" Mama Bear wanted to know.

"How can we stop it?" Baby Bear asked.

"Very simple," I said. "You need to quit hiring detectives to come over here and investigate your porridge, your chairs, and your beds. If you had left well enough alone today you would still have the porridge you liked, the chairs you ordered and your beds, the way you like them. Take my advice, and you'll be happy. I can send you a bill in the morning, or we can settle right now for a couple of jugs of your fine honey. I couldn't help but notice your beehives."

The Wolf Wood Estates Caper

The phone rang on my desk at the Bear With Us Detective Agency. I answered it on the first ring. There was a gruff voice on the other end.

"I'm looking for Detective Bearstone Blackie. This is Mayor Bear Nays from the City of El Bruno."

You're speaking to him, Mayor Nays, I said. "What can I do for you?"

"The city needs a sharp guy like you to find out why we're getting reports of trouble coming out of the Wolf Wood Estates neighborhood."

"Trouble?" I asked. "What sorts of trouble?"

"I'm getting it from both sides," Mayor Nays said. "The owner says tenants of his are trashing the buildings and refusing to pay the rent when he comes to collect. The tenants are saying the buildings are poorly built and that the owner is using scare tactics to collect the rent."

"This sounds like a job for Bearstone Blackie," I said. "Give me all the names, and I'll get to the bottom of this case right away."

Mayor Nays had the list ready when I got to his office. He had made his fortune selling mustard and ketchup before becoming mayor. His campaign slogan was "Not

Mustard, Not Ketchup, But Mayor Nays." He got the vote of nearly every sandwich and coleslaw lover in the city.

I thanked him for the chance to serve our fair city.

"Just remember, Bearstone," he said, "All the folks on this list are sandwich lovers and voters."

My first stop was the downtown office of Wolfram T. Wolf, the owner of Wolf Wood Estates.

"I'm glad we're getting some action from Mayor Nays," Wolfram said. "I try to provide for my tenants in the way they want to be treated, but I think the whole thing has backfired in my face. Help yourself to some of our coffee and donuts."

I nodded and took a chocolate donut.

"Take the case of Kalua D. Pig," Wolfram said. "He's from the Hawaiian Islands. I wanted him to feel at home, so I asked him what kind of a house would he feel comfortable living in?"

I nodded again and took a French donut.

"Without so much as a blink, Kalua says he wants to live in a little grass shack like he did in some place called Kealakekua. So, I say okay. I'll have one of my guys come over with the materials you need, and you two can put it together. This Kalua guy's a musician, so I figure I'll take a chance. He says he's a violinist, but I figure him for a fiddler. Maybe he's what they call a busker, someone who plays on the street and gets coins tossed into his hat. Well, you can see, Mr. Bearstone, Wolf Wood Estates is not exactly Park Avenue."

I nodded. This time I had a croissant.

"Couple days go by, and Kalua has his new grass shack, and he even has the first month's rent. He tells me he's working with another musician, a guy named Hamilton Hog who plays the flute. Hog is looking for his own place, but he doesn't like the grass shack so much. It bothers his allergies. I tell him that we'll look at the budget and see what we can come up with."

"Did you find an answer?" I asked.

"Yeah, I called Mayor Nays. He said he knew of a pool cue manufacturer that was going out of business. I could pick up all the cues for a song. With a tube of Titan Glue and a few extras Hog could be living in the sticks. He'd have a home and I'd make a few dollars. Happy all around, no?"

I nodded and sipped my latte.

"A couple of months go by, and it turns out that these two jokers are a couple of deadbeats that don't have the rent, but want to throw wild parties until all hours. I'm getting complaints from people who live down the road. They can't take any more. Here, take this address."

He handed me the business card of Henry Swine, Contractor, Bricklaying our specialty.

"This guy lives right down the road from the two deadbeats. He's a hard working guy. He and his wife are great people. Petunia used to work in comics and cartoons. Now she runs that little cafe across from city hall.

"They have great sandwiches there," I said.

"So, I kept getting complaints from neighbors," Wolfram said. "I decided I'd go out there one night and see for myself. I get to the little grass hut, and there's nothing but a vacant lot. I go up the road to the next guys place, and there's a huge bonfire and a loud party. The grass shack and the stick house are in the fire and this out of control group is roasting marshmallows and all-beef hot dogs. The two deadbeats are playing loud music, and all the neighbors are yelling that they're going to call the cops."

"What happened then?" I asked.

"I grabbed a garden hose and started squirting out the fire. I got so mad I started squirting everyone at the party. The two deadbeats ran toward Henry Swine's place. He was out in his front yard chasing them off with a shovel, but Petunia was standing at the open front door. That's when they ran past her and took her hostage. They locked the front door. Henry and I stood there in shock. We had to get in. Poor Petunia."

"Wow," I said. I grabbed another donut.

"So Henry boosted me up onto the roof of his brick house. I figured I'd surprise them by going down the chimney. I'm thin. The wife has me on one of those caveman diets. Well, it turns out I wasn't thin enough. I got stuck. Henry had to get a piece of his heavy equipment, a crane to get me out. By that time, Petunia had gotten the better of the two deadbeats by offering them real work as busboys at her café. They couldn't take it. They opened the front door and ran off."

I thanked Wolfram and headed out to Wolf Wood Estates.

I got to the lot where the grass hut had stood. It was empty. The neighbor from across the road came up next to me.

"I hope they never build another one of those grass shacks here," he said. "I told them when they were building it. Same for that one up the road made from pool cues. I told them it was poor construction, but they wouldn't listen. They just kept eating donuts."

I nodded.

"Yeah, I told them we get a lot of wind around here. One huff or one puff would blow those houses down. I told the tenants, too. Went and knocked on their doors and told them. A huff and a puff would blow their house down. They slammed the door in my face."

I nodded.

"That poor Mr. Wolfram," the neighbor said. "He tried to give those two a break and they ended up burning down the houses because they didn't want to pay the rent."

I told the neighbor that I was headed over to see Henry Swine.

"Don't think he's home," the neighbor said. "He's remodeling that old pool cue factory for the mayor. It's going to be a donut factory."

The Jack-of-All-Trades Caper

The phone rang on my desk at the Bear With Us Detective Agency. I answered it on the first ring. There was a concerned voice on the other end.

"I'm looking for Detective Bearstone Blackie."

I thought I recognized the voice.

"Is this Jill?"

"Yes, I'm afraid Jack is in trouble again. We need your help."

I reached for Jack's file in my desk drawer. It was under a sack of croissants from the El Bruno Hungry Bear Donut Factory.

"What seems to be the trouble?" I asked. I bit into a croissant with Swiss cheese inside.

"He's involved in another one of his schemes out where his mother lives in Allergy Acres. Could you go out there and investigate before he gets in too deep?"

I took down the information.

"I'll call you once I know something," I said and hung up.

"That might take some time," a sultry voice said. "You're always telling the cops you don't know a thing."

It was my gal Friday, Beartina. She slinked her way into my office and sat on the corner of my desk.

"You gonna eat that whole sack of croissants, Sugar? Or are you going to share it with a gal who knows how to take care of you?"

It was no use resisting. I gave her the sack of croissants. I had work to do. I had a file on Jack to read through, and I had to get out to Allergy Acres to investigate. Besides, I had a sack of chocolate donuts in my other drawer.

I watched as Beartina wiggled her way out of my office.

I opened the file on Jack.

On the top was the first time he had gone astray.

In those days he was using the alias Jack B. Nimble. The B stood for Bear. He was running a company that did parachute jumps at major events. He had been one of the first skydiving smoke-eater bears that had trained with the Forest Service. Now he was on his own, and he was trying to make a buck for himself.

He had a good idea, but his timing was off. He was supposed to parachute into Candlestick Park at half time of the 49ers-Raiders game. Unfortunately, his plane was delayed in taking off. He ended up landing on the Raiders' quarterback as he was running for a touchdown with two seconds left in the tied game. The ensuing riot brought police from four counties before things settled down.

The papers the next day had headlines about how Jack B. Nimble tried to jump over Candlestick and ruined the game. He went into hiding after that.

When he finally surfaced, he had changed his name and had taken on Jill as a partner. Together they had a show on channel 47. He was Jack Sprat, the Gourmet Chef. It was a cooking show that let the watcher decide whether they wanted to be on a strict diet or to just throw caution to the wind and indulge in exotic deserts and sauces.

Jack Sprat lectured people about too much fat in their diets.

"Celery is a wonderful main course," Jack would say. "Serve it with unsweetened tea and bottled water and bon appetit."

Jill encouraged the audience to avoid lean cuisine.

"Sugar, fat, and alcohol are the holy trinity of gourmet dining," she would say. "Remember, sixty million French people can't be wrong."

The show didn't last long with the two arguing constantly. Jack ended up in the hospital with malnutrition, while Jill finally solved her diet pill addiction at the Betty Ford Clinic.

No more was heard from them until they filed a lawsuit against the Russian Hill Merchants Association. It seems that Jack and Jill had gone to one of the open-air festivals on top of Russian Hill.

"We were interested in trying that new bottled water," Jill said. "Pale Water, they called it. They were giving it away as samples, but the stand was on a slope, and it got very wet from all the spillage. Jack started to slide. I tried to grab him, and we both went tumbling down the hill. Jack hit the crown of his head. He was in rehab for a long time. I don't know if he'll ever be fully recovered."

I had heard that they had settled out of court for a tidy sum that could have kept them in fancy pastry for a long time.

I made my way out to Allergy Acres where Jack's mother, Ursa lived. She was happy to see me.

"Bearstone, Jill called and said you were coming to help," she said. "Maybe you can straighten out this mess. Sit down. I made you some Cottleston pie."

I sat and ate while she talked.

"I've been raising livestock out here, and it just got to be too much," she said. "Jack said he could make a deal. Get rid of all the cows and sheep and turn it into some income property for us. I told him to go ahead. I'd like the extra cash. Maybe I could take a trip to the Bearhamas."

I nodded and had a question for her.

"Do you have any coffee to go with this pie?"

She made the coffee and went on with her tale.

"Almost overnight, this large building sprang up. Jack had traded the animals, and it was like someone had sowed magic beans. I don't even think he pulled a building permit. Anyhow, it's out there, and if you climb up to the top floor, you'll see some crazy Jamaican named Rochester Bear living up there. He's one of Jack's deadbeat friends. No one else wants to live in the place. Jack had the place painted green. The neighbors are calling it a beanstalk. I'm calling it a pain in the you-know-what."

She told me she was worried about collecting the rent. Jack kept visiting the tenant, hoping to collect some money, but he never brought any back home. I finished my coffee and pie and decided it was time to go into action.

It was a sixth-floor walk-up. I finally got to the top and knocked on the door. A big fat guy came to the door. He looked rough, but he was nothing I couldn't handle.

I told him I was representing Ursa and that Jack was out of town.

"Come in, Mon," he said. "How about an omelet? I've got a goose here that lays eggs with a golden colored yolk. Not like that junk you buy at the store."

He was right. It was delicious.

"You know," he said after we ate, "I'm worried about our friend Jack. I've been giving him the rent money, and he keeps using it for this invention of his. He works on it up here at night.

"Invention?" I asked.

16

"Yeah, he calls it a magic harp. It's supposed to play any song you want to hear, any time you want it."

He pointed to it. It sat on a table in the corner. There were dozens of parts strewn about next to a soldering iron and a blowtorch. The magic harp was big and made out of beautiful wood and metal.

"Jack has tried taking it around to guitar shops to see what they think. He starts the harp playing and all of a sudden they aren't interested. It only plays one song, 'Stairway to Heaven.' He can't get the magic harp to play anything else. You don't think it's haunted, do you, Bearstone?"

A haunted harp that only played 'Stairway to Heaven.' That was enough for me. I excused myself and left. I told Ursa where the money had gone from the rent Jack had collected. She was furious but grateful that I had done my gumshoe work.

"Bearstone," she said. "Answer me this: suppose that building was heavily insured and something happened to it. What do you think?"

I told her that she could buy a bunch of donuts with the money, a great big bunch of donuts. Maybe even the El Bruno Hungry Bear Donut Factory.

I didn't hear anything about Jack for a while. Six months went by. I received a postcard from the Bearhamas. It was from Ursa.

"Rochester and I are very happy down here," she wrote. "The sweet bread is wonderful. The insurance payment was even better."

A week later, I finally tracked down Jill to see what she knew about Jack.

Jack's had some mental problems," she said. "He got all upset when his building collapsed, and his mother ran off with Rochester. I'm afraid he's back in the funny box. Keeps talking about a haunted harp. If he hears the song 'Stairway to Heaven,' he jumps out at you like he's spring loaded. Most days he just sits in the corner eating his pudding pie. He sticks his thumb into it and says he's pulling out a plum. Good trick. Not a plum in it. Then he says something about being a good boy. "

I told her I understood.

She had more to say.

"I just couldn't take it the other day," she said. "He was totally out of control. I yelled, 'You've gone crackers, Jack.' Now they've got him wearing a mask over his face to prevent him from biting people. His red bloodshot eyes stare out at you. He looks just like a Halloween pumpkin."

I told her I hoped things would get better. I had to hang up and deal with an important matter.

Beartina and I were spending two weeks with Ursa and Rochester aboard their yacht in the Bearhamas. They were about to serve the Key Lime Pie.

The R&R Caper

The phone rang on my desk at the Bear With Us Detective Agency. I answered it on the first ring.

"Bearstone Blackie. How can I help you?"

There was a gruff voice on the other end.

"Bearstone, It's Wolfie. What's the word? What did you find out?"

"Wolfie. I just got back from checking out those complaints you received from your properties out in Allergy Acres."

I reached for a cheese Danish and a sip of my triple latte.

"Yeah, what happened out there with whatshername, the blonde? You make any headway?"

"Rapunzel you mean?"

"Yeah. What's the story?"

"Same old same old," I said. "She's a quiet tenant. Gets along with the old dame downstairs and then something happens. All of a sudden she lets her hair down and the next thing you know she's carrying on with her latest prince until all hours.

Old Dame Gothel downstairs says her upstairs neighbor is headed for trouble. Gothel says she gets so mad sometimes, she'd like to hide upstairs and toss one of those so-called princes out the window so she could get some peace. 'There's some nice thorny bushes they could land in,' she said."

"You get things settled down?" Wolfie asked.

"For now, anyways. I told Rapunzel if it kept up you'd raise her rent."

"Good move. What did she say to that?"

"She said it was too high now. That's when old Dame Gothel told her to go try living in the woods and see if she liked it better. 'All that long unruly hair of yours draws all these shiftless bums,' she said. 'Get your hair styled into a professional look and you might get a decent man.' "

"You get the rents from those two?"

"Right here in my hand-tooled, Corinthian leather pastry valise, next to the Prune Danish."

"Great, what happened at the other place?"

"More domestic strife, another cute blonde and another bum who thinks he's a prince," I said. I reached for a jelly donut for this one.

"They pay the rent?" Wolfie asked. "Any damage to the apartment?"

"Yeah, no problem there. The blonde's husband is a king when it comes to money. It's the lunatic who keeps stalking her, claiming their kid is really his. She denies it. He wants custody of the kid. She says the only thing she and Nutso ever did together was make spun gold jewelry."

"That's a new way to put it," Wolfie said.

"No, they really made spun gold jewelry," I said. "You can tell she'd never go for this loser. This guy looks like Godzilla on a bad day."

"This is the same guy who goes nuts every time he shows up?" Wolfie asked.

"One and the same, I told him we'd put a temporary restraining order on him to keep him away from Blondie and your property. The wise guy says, 'How you gonna do that? You don't even know my real name?' I looked at his tattooed arms and said, 'I don't think it's Guns, God, and Glory, so it must be Rumpelstiltskin.'"

"What did he do then?" Wolfie asked.

"He ran to his old jalopy and sped off leaving a trail of blue oil smoke. I ran his plates. He lives in some dumpy cottage up in Mountain Woods."

"Good riddance. Did you make it out to see my niece Beau and her talented boyfriend?"

"Baa Baa Black Sheep Farm is doing fine," I said. "I asked Beau if she had any wool for you and she said she had three bags full. I have them here in my office. She says you've been looking forward to wearing a sweater made from sheep's wool."

"She's right, Bearstone. I don't know about you bears, but wolves are absolutely nuts about wearing sheep's designer clothing. How's her boyfriend doing?"

"He had the sheep grazing out in the meadow, and the cows were eating some corn to fatten them up. He's been practicing his trumpet playing, and he has a gig at a new place called Under the Haystack. He's calling himself Little Boy Blues."

"Those kids work hard," Wolfie said. "Farming and a career in music. How do they do it? That kid is great. Beau is fantastic, too. You never hear a peep from her."

"Sharp kids," I said. "Beau said she rounds up the sheep by giving them their freedom. 'Leave them alone, and they'll come home, wagging their tails behind them.' She said. Makes sense, no?"

"It does make sense, Bearstone, but I'm going to have to ring off. I promised my better half I'd take her to some garden center to look for Silver Bells and Cockleshells. She says they probably won't have any. I tell her, 'Mary, Mary so contrary, Wolfie will help your garden grow.' Now I'm stuck. Any idea where I can find flowers like that?"

"You could try old MacDonald's Farm And Garden. You'll have to put up with all the barnyard noise and watch where you step," I said. "I've got to run, too. I just got a text from Geppetto, the furniture maker. He needs my help. Says there's a monkey chasing a weasel around his carpenter's bench."

"Geppetto needs to get away from all those fumes in his shop," Wolfie said. "That glue and varnish will have you seeing things. Wasn't he talking to a puppet the other day? Claimed he saw its nose getting longer?"

"Yeah, pretty sad," I said.

"Listen. Bearstone, why don't you and your gal Beartina meet Mary and me later for dinner. You can bring the rent and the wool. I'll treat."

"Sounds good. Where you want to meet?"

"That guy Jay Diddle-Diddle has a new place called The Cat and the Fiddle. It's down on Broadway. We could meet there about eight. They specialize in beef."

"How are the steaks?" I asked.

"Just like the rest of the cow. They're out of this world."

The El Lobo Caper

I was sitting in my office at the Bear With Us Detective Agency, going through my back cases. With so much crime to deal with in El Bruno, it was hard to keep track. I had worked my way through the alphabet up to the Ps.

There it was: Piper, Peter. He had tried to play it cool. He hid the stolen goods in the trunk of his car and tried to ease through the gate at the Bear Nays Mustard and Ketchup factory.

Like no one would catch on, no one would smell pickled peppers? He didn't count on Buster T. Dawg's schnuffling schnozzola. It was Buster's first day at the gate after returning from DC where he had been filling in for McGruff the Crime Dog. Nor did Peter Piper ponder my professional police procedures that produced the motive for Peter pilfering the peck of purloined pickled peppers.

I had tailed Tom-Tom, Piper's son to the El Bruno Farmers Market. His plan was simple: steal a pig and off you run. He even chanted as I followed him down the street.

"To Market, to market to steal a pig, then home again, home again, jiggety-jig."

At home, he had the charcoal pit all set up and had his sign ready to go, "Pipers' Pork Ribs With Pickled Peppers."

It was a slam-dunk case, according to Mayor Nays. The two could either rot in jail for several months or go into partnership with the mayor on the Ribs and Peppers Bistro. The Pipers were proof that certain crimes pay well. The R&P Bistro was a big hit.

The thought of ribs with pickled peppers made me hungry. I dug into my drawer and brought out a plate of donuts with powdered sugar on them. Just then the intercom sounded with Beartina, my gal Friday's voice.

"That actress Queenie Bianca is out here. You know, 'The Fairest of Them All.' She has her tanning expert with her. Should I send them in?"

Queenie entered with her latest facelift. It was the "Caught in the Wind Tunnel" model. This might have been her fifth tuck.

The guy with her had been a leading man a few years back, but rotgut firewater had ruined his voice. He was reduced to non-speaking extras roles: rich man, poor man, beggar man, thief, doctor, lawyer, Indian chief. You get the idea. His name was Rex Tanner, and he was often referred to in the movie press as "The King of Tanning." He sold a line of suntan lotions and ran an annual Venice Beach tanning contest.

They sat in chairs in front of my desk.

I slid the plate of powdered sugar donuts toward them. From the looks of their noses, they had already eaten several powdered donuts on the way to my office.

"What can I do for you?" I asked.

"Neve Bianca," Queenie said. "I need you to find her, Bearstone."

I knew about Neve Bianca. She had been a rising star in Hollywood. She had jet black hair and a pale complexion that producers had gone wild over. She was Queenie's daughter from her marriage to the late Duke Bianca, the Hollywood director. Several years back, she had disappeared.

24

"She said she was getting out of the business three years ago," Queenie said. "Her picture vanished from Casting Central, but now it just came back on their website. They're calling her 'The Fairest of Them All.' That title belongs to me."

"Any idea where she might be?" I asked, munching on a powdered donut.

"That's why I brought the King of Tanning," Queenie said. "Cough it up, Rex."

"Look, I got a general idea, but no exact address," He started out in his squeaky voice, as if he was going to run up the clock and down again. "We were pretty tight back then, she and I, but…"

"What Rex is trying to say is they had a thing together until he found out she was cold as ice when it came to taking care of a man," Queenie said. "Rex came back to Queenie, and he's a happy man."

"Yeah," Rex said. "Neve's heart belonged to only her. Our plan was to head for El Lobo and live on a boat at the Hi-Ho Harbor. She said she had connections on one of the wharfs, but I never got that far. We had a big argument, and she took off. That's the last I ever saw of her.

"Which wharf? Do you remember?"

"Seventy, maybe," Rex squeaked.

He was annoying, this mouse of a man. I wouldn't urge a farmer's wife to take her carving knife to Rex, but if it happened, I could sympathize.

Queenie dropped a couple of Benjamins on my desk, and it was time to say bye-bye. I was glad when they both left.

I told Wolfie T. Wolf about my new case.

"El Lobo, that's practically home to the Wolf family," Wolfie said. "And Neve Bianca, that babe. She was one of my favorite stars. Bearstone, I should come with you. I haven't been there in years."

We arrived in El Lobo just before noon.

"This town has sure changed," Wolfie said.

"You mean it's gotten bigger?"

"No, looks like most people have left town. Pull up to that bum with the Nitro Vino bottle over there. Maybe he can tell us something."

"This used to be a prosperous town," Wolfie said to the bum. "What happened?"

"Big shippers left town. Place fell apart."

"Which way to the wharfs?" I asked.

"I'll help you if you help me," the bum said.

"Okay," I said.

"You go down a mile to the Dell," the bum said. "There's a farm there. Guy's got a wife and a kid. There's a nurse living there, too. There's a cow and a dog and a cat and a rat. The rat steals the cheese, and that's where you two come in, you see? The cheese stands alone. You guys are the big cheese, right? Well, I need a loan. Can you stand me a loan? Ten bucks? A fin? I ain't et in three weeks."

I couldn't follow his train of thought, but I liked the old bum's spirit. I handed him a double sawbuck and a couple donuts. He was grateful.

"You get to the farmer's place and turn right," he said. "The wharfs are a half mile down."

I thanked him and started to drive off.

He was singing a jingle about the Hi-Ho Dairy as we left.

We got to the wharf area in a few minutes. It looked like there were eight wharves in all, so much for Rex Tanner's guess at seventy. Wharves A, B, and H had fallen into the bay. C and F were in bad shape. Wharves D and E were up and running. They had been remodeled and were filled with small shops and restaurants.

"Well, I don't see any Wharf Seventy," Wolfie said. "Did we get a bum steer from the tanning king?"

I was about to answer him when two Harleys roared up the road and parked next to my Thunder Bear Growler.

There was no mistaking. When she took off her helmet, it could only be one person. Neve Bianca stood next to us in all her beauty. The guy next to her looked familiar, too when he took off his helmet.

"It's Doc Holliday," Wolfie said. "He's in all those action thrillers, The Bourne Appendix, The Scum of All Fears, The Stunt for Dead October."

We watched the two walk down Wharf D and turn into unit 7. It was a motorcycle shop. We followed them in.

"Can I interest you two gents in a new Harley," Doc Holliday asked as we entered.

"It would be fun," I said, "But we're here on different business. I'm Detective Bearstone Blackie. This is my associate Wolfram T. Wolf. We're here to make certain that Neve is safe and sound. Her mother Queenie Bianca hired me. She's worried about her. She hasn't heard from her in three years."

"Ah, yes Queenie," Neve said. "She's probably more worried about the attention she won't be getting when another Bianca re-enters the movie game."

"Maybe so," I said. "She cared enough to force Rex to tell us which town you might be living in. Neither one of them has much of a career left in films. Maybe a few cameos."

"That will happen to all of us," Doc said. "That's why we've gone into the motorcycle business, a life and an income outside of movies."

"So Rex and Queenie are still propping each other up," Neve said. "I guess they're made for each other, but not for me. Around him, I always felt frozen, like I should be in one of those glass display cases you see at the butcher shop. And around her, I always felt like we were competing to be the fairest of them all."

"You should tell these two gents what you're planning to do," Doc said. He reached into an ice chest and pulled out four bottles of root beer and handed one to each of us.

"I've got a three picture deal with Warners," Neve said. "The Girl With the Razor Tattoo, The Hornets Who Played With Fire, and The Girl Who Kicked Over the Dragon. So, you see, Bearstone, I won't be competing with Queenie for the fairest title. She can have that."

"Tell him about your name," Doc said. "It will make a big impression on your mother."

"I'm going to Anglicize my name," she said. "No more Neve Bianca. Queenie can have Bianca to herself. Here's my new card."

The card read:
Snow White
Hi-Ho Harleys
7 D Wharf
El Lobo, CA

I handed her my cell phone.

"Please press call and talk to Queenie?" I asked. "Just for a minute. I want her to know you're okay."

She paused a moment, then took the phone and smiled her famous smile at me.

The minute took an hour and a half, during which it was decided that Queenie would always be The Fairest and Snow would always be The Edgiest. Hi-Ho Harleys would be one of the sponsors of the Venice Tanning Tournament, with Doc Holliday and Bearstone Blackie as two of the judges. Also, Rex and Queenie would get walk-on parts in The Girl With the Razor Tattoo.

It was a touching scene with smiles and tears, many coming from Wolfie who had discovered his inner biker. Doc Holliday made the Wolf street legal that afternoon, selling him a Harley Superlow, and of course a helmet and a black leather jacket.

The back of the jacket read, "Wolves Love HOGS, Hi-Ho Harley, El Lobo, California."

How could any wolf resist?

The Faux Fox Fawkes Caper

The phone rang on my desk at the Bear With Us Detective Agency. I answered it on the first ring. There was a sultry female voice on the other end.

"I'm looking for Detective Bearstone Blackie. I need his help."

"You're speaking to him. How can I help?"

"The name's Little. Muffet Little. I run a place called the C&W in the Bottom Dollar Gulch section of town. I want to talk to you about stopping a big crime in its tracks. You're the best around. I've seen you on TV."

I took down her information and packed six cannoli into my hand-tooled Corinthian leather pastry valise and headed down to one of the seedier parts of town. I parked my Thunder Bear Growler on a side street and walked over to the run-down C&W on Smokey Bear Row.

With a name like C&W, I figured it would be a country and western joint with loud, twangy music playing. I was wrong. It was a pleasant little café inside with customers sitting on tuffets enjoying the specialty of the house, curds, and whey.

"Bearstone," someone yelled as I entered. "Come back here."

She was a cute blonde dressed in a frilly white apron partly covering her blue jumper. I sat down on a tuffet across from her. I had a clear view of the room. She noticed me watching the door.

"You expecting trouble, Bearstone?" Muffet asked.

"Not particularly," I said. "But if it stumbles through that door, I'm ready for it."

"I'm ready, too Bearstone. I used to be afraid of spiders. Imagine that. But I've gotten tougher. This neighborhood has gone to the dogs."

I nodded.

"Take that group of losers over there." She pointed toward a group of four sitting around a table. "That's the Porker Brothers. All they do is complain about each other. Listen to them."

She was right. They were loud and crude. The fat guy in the group said he was fed up with the rest of them.

"How come it's always me going to the market?" he asked.

"Quit breakin' my chops," the guy next to him said. "You think it's a picnic staying home? The glutton over here eats all the roast beef in the place and then Junior the prince complains all day that he has none. And what about Pinky? Where'd he go?"

"He's squealing, running home to Ma," the fat guy said. "Can't you hear him going wee wee wee all the way home?"

I noticed a couple oddballs sitting together at the counter. One guy looked like an over-dressed mambo instructor. The other guy had a cast on his arm and bruises on his face.

"Who's the guy eating pudding and pie and who's the mug with him?" I nodded toward them. "Are they the big crime wave you want me to stop?"

"No, they're just small time hustlers," Muffet said. "Georgie Porgie thinks he's God's gift to women, a real love 'em and cheat 'em type. Kiss the babes and make 'em cry. The guy next to him is a small time thief. Goes by the name Goosey Gander. Cops caught him in a mansion up in El Bruno, wandering upstairs, downstairs and in a lady's chamber. One of the cops told him to say his prayers. Grabbed him by the leg and threw him down the stairs."

I nodded.

A well-dressed woman sat by herself in a booth. She had shopping bags from Tiffany's, Nordstrom and Neiman Marcus.

"The woman with all the gold jewelry, what's her story?"

"You want the latest version?" Muffet asked.

I nodded.

"Poor Mrs. Gantry went to the pantry to get her poor poodle a bone. When she got there, the pantry was bare..."

"Wait a minute," I said. "Haven't I heard a different version of this story?"

"Sure," Muffet said. "There's the Old Mother Hubbard version where she goes to the cupboard; there's the Old Mrs. Ridge who goes to the fridge, the Old Mrs. Harder who goes to the larder, the Old Mrs. Caesar who goes to the freezer. She usually has four or five identities going. Between the phony credit cards and the government welfare agencies, she does great."

"So, she must be the one-woman crime wave you called me here for?"

"No. I'd have to be nuts to do that," Muffet said. "She's supporting half the businesses down here in Bottom Dollar Gulch. I brought you down here to talk about Guy Fawkes."

"Some guy named Fox?" I asked. "Some fox named Guy?"

"Guy Fawkes. They have a night for him in downtown El Bruno. It's just after Halloween. All the kids will make Guy Fawkes scarecrows to set on fire. There'll be fireworks and games. It's a big deal."

"So where's the big crime in that?"

"The FOOF is running the event."

"FOOF?"

"Yeah, the Fraternal Order of Foxes is running Guy Fawkes Night. They're going to have a large marching band followed by a hundred marching foxes, all dressed up like Guy Fawkeses."

"Foxes dressed like Fawkeses?"

"Yeah, except one of them will be a faux fox dressed like Fawkes."

"This doesn't have anything to do with fee, fi, fo, fum, does it?"

"No. It's faux not fo. Anyhow the faux fox dressed like Fawkes will sneak into city hall and do what the original Guy Fawkes failed to do in London."

"Which is?"

"Blow the place up with gunpowder."

I looked around the room to see if anyone was listening.

"How do you know this to be true?" I asked.

"The proof is that the FOOF has their meetings here at the C&W every Friday afternoon. Before every meeting, I get faxes of the foxes planning to attend. Last Friday one fox fax had a faux fox listed for the Fawkes fest meeting."

"You mean a fake fox was in the faux Fawkes fox fax?"

"The fax came from the El Fuego Cigar and Blasting Powder Factory. That's what it said on the letterhead. It was signed Farnsworth T. Fox, but on the top of the letterhead it said Shyster T. Wolf."

I told her what I knew about Shyster T. Wolf.

He was the black sheep of the Wolf family and the nephew of Wolfram T. "Wolfie" Wolf who owned rental properties around El Bruno. Wolfie knew that Shyster wasn't the sharpest knife in the drawer. El Bruno police frequently caught him selling stolen chickens at the farmers market. One arresting officer said he knew something was wrong with Shyster's act.

"Usually, you take the feathers off the bird before you barbecue it," the cop said.

Wolfie tried to do right by Shyster. He hired him to collect some of the rents on his properties. Shyster got in trouble again out at Betty Hood's mobile home. She had a granddaughter, Red who kept riding Shyster. Why couldn't he spend some of that rent money with her? She'd show him a good time.

There was a catch -- Granny Betty didn't want Red hanging out with the likes of Shyster.

"Honey," Granny said to Red, "We may be trailer trash, but he's even trashier. He's barnyard trash."

One day Shyster went to collect the rent, and he figured he could kill two birds with one stone. He grabbed Granny Betty and locked her in the closet. He jumped into her Queen size bed and waited for Red to show up. Too bad for Shyster that Red showed up with her date for the hour, a burly lumberjack named Thor. Luckily for Shyster, his pathetic imitation of Granny Betty got everyone laughing so hard he was able to make it out of the place alive.

Shyster got lucky again when he hooked up with the Central Intelligence Agency. The CIA had been looking for a guy who knew how to steal chickens and lock up grannies in closets. They figured that Shyster was a natural to make exploding Cuban cigars. El Fuego Cigar and Blasting Powder Factory was born.

Shyster thought he could save money by renting out the basement of city hall for his business, but Mayor Nays and the city council said no.

"No way do I want that chicken-thieving, granny-terrorizing, bomb-maker anywhere near city hall," Mayor Nays said.

"Talking about chickens," Shyster said. "I sent the mayor a box of my cigars to show no hard feelings. Now he's too chicken to light one."

I turned to Muffet. She was worried.

"A faux fox dressed as Fawkes is going to blow up city hall, Bearstone. We've got to do something."

I told her not to worry. I'd call a few people.

In minutes it was all under control.

When Shyster T., the faux fox dressed as Fawkes stepped out of the FOOF parade with a box of El Fuegos in hand, Granny Betty was waiting with Thor's lumberjack ax.

"Locking me in my closet was an insult, son," she said. "But stealing my chickens, that's a capital offense."

She chased Shyster all the way to the rail yard where he jumped into a moving boxcar loaded with loose straw. The train picked up speed, leaving Granny Betty in the dust.

Shyster smiled. He was out of danger.

He could relax. He was way too clever for Granny Betty and Bearstone Blackie.

Without so much as a thought, he lit an El Fuego and leaned back.

The Flashdark Caper

I was sitting in my office at the Bear With Us Detective Agency, reading the El Bruno Gazette. The stories got crazier every day.

A guy was caught cheating at a walking marathon. There it was in the sports section. "Crooked man walks crooked mile." The story went on to describe how officials discovered he had taken a payoff. He claimed he had "found" the money on a turnstile. There was even something crooked about the title to the guy's house.

In another story, El Bruno Police were looking for an old man who was running around the downtown area assaulting people. A woman quoted in the article said, "This old fool comes running up to me and says he's going to play knick-knack on my knee. That's when I hit him with my umbrella. He starts in mumbling something about a paddywhack. I gave him a good paddywhack. And then he says he's going to give a dog a bone. Well, I ain't no dog. I hit him again. Just another drunk, rolling home, if you ask me."

In another story, thieves had taken an elegant coach with horses from a society ball. In their place, the culprits left a carved pumpkin with mice inside.

"I remember looking out on the driveway just before midnight. The coach was there," said society patron Sonny Duke, heir to the Duke, Duke, Duke, Duke & Earl fortune. "I was dancing with a beautiful woman. She said she needed to excuse herself. I noticed that her shoe had slipped from her foot. I bent to pick it up. When I looked up, the coach was gone."

Police were searching suspected chop shops in the area for the elegant coach, believed to be valued over two hundred thousand dollars. They were also making inquiries at area butcher shops for remnants of the horses.

An item near the bottom of the page caught my eye. The headline on the story read, "Mysterious Shadow Floats Through Downtown El Bruno."

Beneath the headline was a slightly out of focus photo of a triangular shadow, wide at the bottom, thin at the top. Sticking out of the top of the shadow was what looked like a hairy hand holding a metallic object. I read more:

"Frightened shoppers ran for cover when a mysterious black triangle with a large furry hand sticking out of the top of it chased people to the safety of shops and offices. The shape made its way past the Bear Nays Mustard and Ketchup Factory toward the El Bruno Hungry Bear Donut Factory where it suddenly disappeared. Officials from El Bruno have reportedly contacted NASA and Homeland Security in efforts to determine the origin of the dark shape and the degree of any threat posed by the object."

It was enough to make me reach for another chocolate cannoli. Just then my gal Friday, Beartina walked into my office.

"I'm heading over to Costco to buy printer ink and have lunch. I'll trust you not to destroy the place while I'm gone."

I watched her wiggle out the door, on her way to sample her way through lunch.

I leaned back in my swivel chair and took a swig of my triple latte. The world was a crazy place. The El Bruno Gazette certainly had gotten that right.

I heard a small knock on my office door. Whoever it was must have just missed Beartina.

"Mr. Bearstone?" The voice was in our outer office.

"In here," I said. "Come on in."

He was one of those dot.com bears you see hanging around some of the cyber plants in Cinnamon Valley. He wore a black tee shirt and faded jeans and carried a large laptop case.

"I need your help, Mr. Bearstone."

I told him to sit down and make himself comfortable.

"Just call me Bearstone," I said, reaching to shake his hand.

"Uh, Grizz Lee Bearloft. You can call me Grizz if you'd like."

"Okay, Grizz," I said. "Have a seat."

He settled into his chair. I slid a plate of cannoli toward him. He took one of the mint flavored ones.

"What's your story, Grizz?"

"I'm an innovator. I run a shop called Honey Ware Industries. Ever since I was a cub, I've been inventing things. I always say necessity is the mother of invention. If enough demand is there, the invention follows. That's how I ended up inventing the Frozen Banana Icy with the Hot Fudge Center. Kids wanted it, and I found a way to do it. Technology delivers."

"Great invention," I said. "I love that product. How can that be any trouble?"

"It's not. It's my newest invention that I'm concerned about."

"What's that?"

He looked around the room and then at me. There was desperation in his manner. Finally, he spoke.

"It's the FlashDark," he mumbled.

"The FlashDark? Like Flash and Dark? What's it do? Is it a secret weapon?"

"I hope not," he said. "It's meant to help, not hurt. It could revolutionize the way society functions. There was demand for it."

"Like for the Frozen Banana Icy with the Hot Fudge Center?"

"Yeah. A lot of bears wrote to me saying that they were tired of getting stung every time they'd visit their local beehive. During the day bees are active. At night, they pretty much go to sleep. I figured what these bears needed was instant nighttime, something they could carry with them in their purse or pockets. The FlashDark works that way."

"Enlighten me," I said.

"Not much to it," Grizz said. "It's just reverse engineering the ordinary flashlight to make it shine darkness instead of light at the target. In this case, it was the beehive. A bear could cover the hive with a deep dark shadow while holding the FlashDark with say his left hand and use his right hand to help himself to a honey treat. It's potentially a big hit for Honey Ware Industries."

"But you think there's a problem?"

"A few. If you looked at the initial FlashDark test, you'd see a deep dark cone of shadow floating toward a beehive, but on top of the shadow is a bear's hand sticking out holding the FlashDark. Many people got upset when they'd see this coming along. Think of how frightening something like that could be for kids. Was this a creature from the Black Lagoon? Was it a man from Mars? No, it was only a bear on his way for a honey snack."

"Well, what could you do about that?" I asked, knowing he was the probable cause of El Bruno shoppers running for their lives from black triangles.

"First we tried two FlashDarks. One aimed down at the bear underneath it and the beehive and the other aimed up to where the mysterious hand held the FlashDark. So with one cone of darkness aimed down and the other aimed up, you didn't see the mysterious bear hand holding a

FlashDark. All you saw was a triangle of black aimed down and another aimed up. Together they formed an hourglass shape."

"Did that solve the problem, then?"

"Yes and no. It got the hungry bear to the hive for his snack, but now with both his hands carrying FlashDarks he couldn't reach in and get any honey."

"What did you do then?"

"We developed the cloud umbrella. It clipped onto the FlashDark and looked like a small cloud. The FlashDark was now aimed upward into the cloud umbrella and reflected back down to form the dark cone. So now the bear could have one hand holding the FlashDark with the special cloud umbrella attachment and still have one hand free to snack from the beehive. It could be a huge success. Beekeepers and bears all over the world could be using it."

He had a billion dollar baby, and he was worried.

"What else can the FlashDark be used for?" I asked.

"Too much sun on a sunny day is not good for a nap in a hammock. Many of our customers could solve that problem by hanging a FlashDark above their favorite afternoon napping place. You can adjust the level of darkness coming from the FlashDark. This would allow folks to have candlelight dinners in the middle of the sunniest days. I'm even working on a colossal model that would allow a city to turn it on and have a fireworks display in the middle of the day. No more making kids stay up past their bedtime to see the skyrockets."

"And you're worried?"

"Plenty. Yesterday, I took a walk with it past the mustard and ketchup plant and walked over to the donut place. If you read the Gazette today or saw the news on Channel 8, you'd swear that we had been invaded by terrorists or Martians. I don't want this device to be an instrument of destruction. Bank robbers might use the

FlashDark. I wouldn't put it past a crooked politician to use a FlashDark to steal an election or start another war."

"Yeah, I heard about your trip to the donut shop, Grizz. What were you thinking?"

"I was thinking about those lemon custard-filled donuts with colored sprinkles on top, but I also was experimenting. Seeing how people would react to seeing it. It was pretty brutal the way people ran away from me."

I nodded.

"So, what can I do?" I asked.

"I want you to evaluate the FlashDark out in the field," he said. "You do a lot of different cases. I want full reports from you about how the FlashDark might be useful without being a danger to our way of life. Maybe this is something strictly for the government."

"Or maybe it's only for people we can trust," I said.

He opened his laptop case and took out a smaller leather case and placed it on my desk.

"These are your FlashDarks," he said. "The instructions are inside along with the chargers. There's an envelope with a thousand dollars in it. Let me know when you need more."

I stood and shook his hand. In seconds he was out the door. I sat back and opened the case. Both FlashDarks felt heavy in hand, like a well-balanced pistol. I turned one on, and a dark cone covered my office door.

Just then, Beartina walked into my office.

"Why you always acting so cheap?" she asked. "Turn on some lights around here. I don't know how you can work in the dark like that."

I switched off the FlashDark, and things went back to my normal gloomy office décor.

"I'm going back to Costco and buy you a decent lamp," Beartina said. "Besides, they're sampling shrimp tempura, chocolate ice cream, and Polish sausage today."

I dropped the FlashDarks into my desk drawer.

"I better go with you to help you carry stuff," I said.

"We need to buy you a desk lamp and a big, black metal flashlight," Beartina said. "You need to have the up-to-date professional equipment. Who do you think you would impress with that thing you were fooling with when I walked in?"

I smiled.

It was a question I looked forward to answering.

The Sonny Duke Caper

It was mid afternoon. Wolfram T. Wolf sat in a chair facing my desk at the Bear With Us Detective Agency. He looked beat. He had just come from the El Bruno Courthouse where he had testified in what some were calling the "El Bruno Candy House Camp Disaster."

"Those rotten spoiled kids," Wolfie said. "Their parents send them off to an exclusive camp for the summer and what happens? The two snots can't take all the gourmet cuisine that Samantha Greywitch offers at the Candy House Camp, and they take off, supposedly headed for home, but they get lost. Yeah, sure. Lost for two weeks until they finally show up at home, dirty and broke. The camp is four miles from their house. That snotty son of theirs saying, 'What you want me to do, follow bread crumbs to come back to this dump?' Some dump, the Woodsman Estate, fourteen bedrooms, an Olympic size pool with sauna and tennis courts."

I knew the story, and I knew Wolfie was upset. He had been the owner of the property where gourmet chef Samantha Greywitch had set up the camp for kids.

"I told the judge that there was something fishy about the story these kids were telling," Wolfie said. "And something fishy about the way the parents didn't bat an eye at them showing up after two weeks on the road. So what do they do? They send their little darlings right back to Candy House Camp. They get a reward for being out of control. The boy doesn't seem too swift, but the girl, she's thirteen going on 21 and doesn't miss a trick."

"She's the one who tried to shove Samantha Greywitch into the hot oven?" I asked.

"Accused her of being a cannibal and stole her purse, too," Wolfie said. "Ended up burning down the whole lodge. Poor Samantha had to have plastic surgery. She had third-degree burns on her arms and her face. And get this: fancy Nancy Woodsman, the kids' mother gets on the stand and tells the judge, 'My Gretel would never do anything like that.' Meantime, I'm sitting there with a pile of ashes where Candy House Camp used to be. What am I going to do? Sue the oven manufacturer?"

I was about to commiserate some more with Wolfie when Beartina walked into my office and shut the door behind her.

"There's a Sonny Duke that just walked in," she said. "Want me to toss the Wolf out the side door? This Sonny guy looks like he's loaded with dough."

"No, the Wolf stays," I said. "I want Wolfie to stick around and listen to what this guy has to say. The Wolf might be helping me on special assignments."

"Lord knows, he can use some money since his camp was burnt to the ground," Beartina said. "He going to sit on the sofa like the Hawk does in all those Spenser for Hire stories?"

"Excellent idea." I nodded.

Wolfie moved to the sofa.

"Yo do ah gots ta jive in Ebonics, too?" Wolfie asked.

"Maybe Wolfonics will do," I said. "Send Sonny in. We'll hear what he has to say."

Sonny Duke walked in and sat down. He was a walking Fortune 500 listing, definitely not the type you offered a cannoli to, maybe a crumpet, but my desk drawers were fresh out of crumpets.

"What can I do for you?" I asked.

He looked at me and then at the Wolf sitting on my designer Salvation Army hide-a-bed in genuine Naugahyde.

"Don't worry," I said. "He's had all his shots. The Wolf does some of the heavy lifting around here when needed."

"I'll come right to the point," Sonny Duke said. "You heard about what happened at my ball last night?"

"Yeah, someone heisted your carriage and a couple of tons of horse meat."

"I don't care about that," Sonny said. "The El Bruno cops can spend their time chasing that stuff down. Frankly, none of it belonged to me. I want you to find the girl I was with when the thievery went down. I know you're good, Mr. Bearstone. Money's no object. Here's two thousand bucks to get started on. All I can tell you is she's a beautiful blonde; I think her name might be Ella and she lost this slipper right before the carriage got stolen."

He placed a glass slipper on my desk.

He handed me a copy of the invitation to his ball and a list of guests in attendance. In five minutes he was gone.

Wolfie was quick to react.

"Yo Sonny can't remember da ho's name, but he strolls in here wif uh glass slipper an' expects us ta pull off uh magic trick? You know das right?

"Wolfie," I said. "In English, please."

"Sorry, Bearstone. I slipped into that Avery Brooks/Hawk role way too easy. What I meant to say was, he wants us to find that girl, and he's not sure of her name? All he's got is her shoe?"

"We've got some leads from his guest list and invitation. I know who we want to talk to first."

The Pipe and Bowl was one of the classiest clubs in El Bruno. It was owned and operated by one of the legends of music, a man who single-handedly invented Merry Old Soul music.

King Cole and his Fiddlers Three ensemble had been the featured band at Sonny Duke's ball. With their electronically enhanced amplifiers and effects units, the four artists could replicate and out-do almost any sound around, but they were known for Merry Old Soul music. The group had just finished their afternoon rehearsal when Wolfie and I walked in. Kenny, the bartender, pointed us to a table where the group sat taking a break.

"Bearstone, Baby," Old King said. "I see you got my favorite Wolf with you. This must be about what went down last night at Sonny Duke's bash."

"Yeah, we saw Sonny earlier this afternoon at my office," I said. "He wants us to find the girl he was dancing with when the carriage and horses got swiped."

I showed him the glass slipper.

"That's what she was wearing, all right. We were out on the veranda, serenading all the lovers at the witching hour. Quite a crew of eligible bachelors and fine looking women. Sonny and that gal weren't exactly dancing at the time. She had that glass slipper on one foot, but she was one piece up on Sonny. I don't think he even had his Rolex on."

"So, what do you know about her?" Wolfie asked. "Ever see her before? Know her name?"

"She likes to party. I know that. Some say she goes by the name Ella. I see her and her sisters at a lot of the dances we play."

"Sisters?" Wolfie asked.

"Marginal looking hustlers," Old King said. "But they manage to hook up. Most of the guys at these events aren't there to get married. They just want a taste."

"Know where we can find this Ella?" I asked.

"If you go to enough parties, she'll turn up. Other than that, can't say." He shrugged.

We left the club and started to walk down the sidewalk when a voice came out of the darkened alley.

"Bearstone, Wolfie, over here. It's Kenny, the bartender."

We walked into the darkened alley.

"Kenny. You in here?" I asked.

"Yeah, I maybe can help you find the gal you're looking for. What's it worth to you?"

"You got a good lead; I'll give you a C-note," I said.

"Okay. It's a good lead, guaranteed."

I handed him the crisp hundred dollar bill.

"The Muffin Man," he said.

"What?" I asked.

"The Muffin Man. Do you know the Muffin Man?"

"The Muffin Man?"

"The Muffin Man?" Wolfie asked.

"Yeah, the Muffin Man," Kenny said. "There some kind of echo in here?"

"Do we know the Muffin Man? Is that what you asked?" I asked.

"Yeah, the Muffin Man on Drury Lane. It's a dive bar. That's where this Ella hangs out with her sisters. Her stepmother Sadie Tremaine runs the joint. You gotta watch out for her. To her, the girls are strictly income property. If you got the money, they got the time."

I called Sonny Duke and told him what we had learned and that we had a line on his Ella. I wanted to know what his intentions were. He was quick to give me the details.

They should have named it Dreary Lane. It was a run-down area. The Muffin Man was the only bright spot on the block with its neon signs. We walked in and noticed a group surrounding a blonde on a barstool. She had one glass slipper on showing it off to the crowd.

"There's another that matches it," she said. "I guess I lost it somewhere."

"Would this do the trick?" I asked, handing her the other glass slipper. "Sonny Duke wants you to try this on."

She looked at me and then at the Wolf.

"You're Bearstone Blackie, and this is the Wolf. I've seen you on TV. Listen, if Sonny is looking for his Rolex, tell him I must have grabbed it by mistake when I was getting dressed. I think I might have his money clip somewhere in my purse, too. Maybe along with his wallet. He's such a passionate man. A poor girl like me just gets all confused around a powerful man like that."

"Sonny has a message for you," I said.

She looked up at me with her blue eyes.

I read from my notes:

"Sonny wants to know that if he were king in his counting house counting all the money, would you be queen in his parlor, eating bread and honey?"

Her cheeks began to blush and a tear trickled from her left eye. She reached into her purse and handed me the wallet and the Rolex.

"Last night with Sonny was unforgettable," she said. "But one night was enough. I'm keeping his money clip. He never paid me, Bearstone. He just wanted to use me. I can't stand to be around dishonest people."

Just then Sadie Tremaine walked up to the group.

"Bearstone and the Wolf," she said. "One of my suppliers just brought in some fresh steaks. Want to take some home, five bucks a pound for the prime cuts?

"Just what cut are they?" Wolfie asked.

"Viande de cheval, very French," she said.

"Nice try," Wolfie said. "I think your steak still owes me six bucks from when I bet on him at Golden Gate Fields."

We called Sonny to tell him his romance with Ella was over.

"Yeah, that line about the counting house and the eating bread and honey rarely works," Sonny said. "Just send me the wallet. You can keep the Rolex, and she can have the clip with the money in it. I gotta run, hot date tonight. That sexy Samantha Greywitch is having me for dinner."

The Slick Willy Jefferson Caper

Wolfram T. Wolf was sitting across the desk from me at the Bear With Us Detective Agency. We had just finished testing the worthiness of vanilla versus chocolate flavored cannoli from the Hungry Bear Donut Factory. As usual, it came out a draw, to be decided later.

"I just can't figure it, Bearstone," Wolfie said. "I bust my bottom to get ahead as a rental property owner, and what happens? I let most of it ride on a deal for the Candy House Summer Camp, and I lose it all. And then there's my nephew Shyster. How do you figure?"

No one could forget the image of Shyster T. Wolf, dressed in his Guy Fawkes costume, running away from Granny Betty Hood who was swinging an ax in his direction. The chase went from El Bruno City Hall to the El Bruno Bearlington Western Railroad Yard where Shyster jumped into a straw-filled boxcar. The train moved slowly away as Granny Betty tried desperately to hang on to the caboose.

"I just can't figure it," Wolfie said. "Some people saw a flash like from a cigar lighter and then came the explosion. Was Shyster that dumb that he didn't realize he was lighting a loaded cigar and carrying a box of the El Fuego Cigar and Blasting Powder Factory Havanas?"

"Not according to his lawyer, Slick Willy Jefferson," I said. "What looked like a disaster turned out to be pure gold for almost everyone involved."

"Yeah, except the railroad," Wolfie said.

I remembered the explosion as the train crossed Bushwhacker Terrace. Someone flew through the side of the boxcar and bounced across the street where they crashed through the window of the Taiwan Ahn Liquor, Gun and Bait Shop. Was it Shyster? Was he dead?

No, on both counts.

It was railroad detective Lionel Bumgrabber, who had been sitting in the boxcar looking for hoboes. The EMTs found him still alive, next to the "Catch More Fish With an AR-15," display.

What had happened to Shyster? Wasn't he there for the explosion? Weren't those his cigars?

Well, that's where attorney Slick Willy Jefferson came into the picture.

Tired of being called an ambulance chaser, Slick Willy had invested in his own ambulance and crew of emergency medical technicians who were on the scene way before the El Bruno EMTs could get out of their Guy Fawkes costumes and get a battery jump from a passing taxi cab.

Slick Willy had the jump on everyone, and he would control the story.

Shyster was found in a drainage ditch beside the tracks. He had managed to put out his smoldering Guy Fawkes costume by diving into the muddy water. Granny Betty Hood was found clinging to the back end of the smoldering caboose. She still had her lumberjack ax in hand. Slick Willy made sure that the photographer for the El Bruno Gazette took a picture of her.

With Granny, Shyster and Bumgrabber transported to El Bruno's Monsanto Memorial Medical Center; Slick Willy called a press conference for the next afternoon.

"This is a terrible way to run a railroad," Slick Willy announced. "I have affidavits from people who have attested from years back about the sorry state of this railroad, an affront to safety and decency. Here's one from a Mr. Jerry Garcia who says someone under the influence of cocaine was driving a train, an engineer by the name of Casey Jones. Another affidavit about how they treat minority workers. A man named John Henry was over-worked so hard laying track, he died with a hammer in his hand. One of their trains on the Rock Island Line is advertised as the road to ride, but the timetable consists of 'if you want to ride it, you got to ride it like you find it.' So much for customer service, health and safety maintenance."

He was just getting started.

"Shyster T. Wolf was dressed in a Guy Fawkes costume, attempting to help the town of El Bruno celebrate a civic occasion. When he saw his train pulling out, he ran for one of the last cars and did his best to jump aboard. Even though there was a railroad employee on that car, Mr. Wolf was given no help. Instead, he was told by Detective Lionel Bumgrabber that there was no smoking allowed in that car. Mr. Wolf gladly handed over the cigar he had just mistakenly lit and made a gift of a box of fifty El Fuego Cigar and Blasting Powder Factory cigars to Detective Bumgrabber to thank him for pointing out the no smoking policy.

"Realizing he was on the wrong train, Mr. Wolf attempted to jump off opposite the side he had boarded. At no time did Detective Bumgrabber attempt to slow the train for Mr. Wolf, or to even point out safe seating and fire control systems. Instead, the lit cigar that Detective Bumgrabber now owned exploded sending sparks into Bumgrabber's private collection of fifty loaded cigars. The explosion of that lot caused the train to derail and catch fire. Rather than staying to assist, Detective Bumgrabber left the scene of the accident and broke into the liquor store across the street from the holocaust."

Camera shutters clicked, and reporters tried to ask questions, but Slick Willy raised his hand and read more from his prepared statement.

"Mr. Wolf was found, nearly drowned in a drainage ditch beside the track." Slick Willy smiled and winked at the young redheaded reporter with the shapely legs and resumed his statement. "The force of the explosion destroyed Mr. Wolf's custom designed Guy Fawkes costume and threw him into the ditch. Fortunately, EMTs on the scene were able to quickly transport him to the hospital. As for Mrs. Betty Hood, affectionately known as 'Granny' to the good folks in El Bruno, she saw the danger and did her best to fight her way through the wreckage to rescue anyone on that train. She suffered smoke inhalation, bruises, and back injuries. She also has been transported to the hospital by the SWJ Ambulance Service."

"What about the railroad dick, Bumgrabber?" A reporter shouted above the noisy crowd. "Is he in the slammer for busting into the liquor store?"

"As far as I know, charges on him are on hold, pending a full investigation," Slick Willy said. "He's being kept under guard in a secure unit at the hospital. We'll know more when he regains consciousness."

The Bearlington Western Railroad wanted a quick settlement with Shyster and Granny. Their own employee had been holding the cigar box full of bombs. There was no doubt that he had been found unconscious in a puddle of gin in the liquor store surrounded by busted bottles. Lots of bucks would make some of the problems go away.

The railroad was owned by Americans Stand Strong Insurance Enterprise which made money by the carload off health insurance policies. ASSIE executives did some calculations. If they raised everyone's premiums by two dollars each month, they'd have plenty of money to pay

Shyster and Granny and still have some left over for year-end bonuses. It was a win-win situation, plus they could use the example of Slick Willy in their attempt to put a ceiling on lawsuits against railroads.

Everything started to move as planned. Shyster and Granny each got a bucket full of money, minus forty percent for Slick Willy.

Meanwhile, Detective Lionel Bumgrabber lay in a coma at Monsanto Memorial Medical Center.

Maybe Bumgrabber would never wake up.

But then one day, he did.

He started to remember what had happened to him on that fateful night that a faux fox dressed as Guy Fawkes tried to climb aboard his train. Bumgrabber smelled a wolf, a shady one at that who had handed him a box of El Fuego Cigar and Blasting Powder Factory cigars. He tried to sit up in bed and noticed that he was handcuffed to a steel bracket on the wall. Bumgrabber knew what had happened. The crummy Bearlington Western Railroad was going to make him the fall guy.

What could he do?

He looked at the cast on his arm. There was a small card taped to it. It read: "Don't be Silly, Call Slick Willy!" Under the type was a phone number.

He called.

Slick Willy had it figured. Lionel Bumgrabber could relax.

In luxury, he could relax.

"I'm so terribly troubled by the way members of the law enforcement community are treated in this country," Slick Willy began his press conference the next afternoon. "The heroics of Detective Lionel Bumgrabber in saving Shyster T. Wolf by showing him a route to safety, have gone for naught in the eyes of his employers. This is another case of a railroad poorly-run, a railroad that can't get it together on its own, but instead attempts to railroad its employees. I have affidavits attesting to Detective Bumgrabber's bravery during the tragic accident. Both the beloved Granny Betty Hood and El Bruno's renowned civic leader Shyster T. Wolf are on record telling how this man saved lives and kept Bearlington Western Railroad, a poorly run railroad from destroying the town of El Bruno."

The railroad caved again. Bumgrabber got a bucket full of money, less forty percent for Slick Willy. Health insurance premiums went up another dollar each month.

Year-end bonuses at the railroad would be even more generous this year.

Two weeks later, the El Bruno Gazette reported that Slick Willy Jefferson had been elected to the board of directors of the Americans Stand Strong Insurance Enterprise.

"ASSIE and Slick Willy Jefferson belong together," said ASSIE president Delbert J. Whiplash. "He understands the modern financial realities we face."

The article went on to say that Slick Willy was the owner of the SWJ Ambulance Service, a member of the board of directors at Monsanto Memorial Medical Center, managing partner at the El Fuego Cigar and Blasting Powder Factory, and owner of the Taiwan Ahn Liquor, Gun and Bait Shop.

The Search for Sonny Duke Caper

Hot winds from the Valley kept the cooling fog out of El Bruno. It was typical of the late summer days that brought most things to a stop. Trying to stay cool was on everyone's mind. The ceiling fan above my desk at the Bear With Us Detective Agency tried its best to cool my office. I sat drinking an iced latte. My assistant gumshoe Wolfie was attempting to stay cool with lemon iced tea. He sat on our neon pink Naugahyde couch as he told me about his latest escapade.

"That case I just had over at the French monastery was a real joke," Wolfie said. "I go over there looking for some guy named Frere Jacques, and it turns out his name is Brother John. There's this big controversy going on. The English muckety-muck in charge says this Brother John guy is ringing the bells too loud. The French guy in charge says this Frere Jacques guy isn't ringing them at all. He's sleeping through his shift, or maybe something happened to him."

"They thought it might be foul play?" I asked.

"Yeah, we went over to the guy's room to get the story. I knock, and he finally comes to the door with a slew of excuses. He says he thought it was raining and pouring too much to go to work. Then he says he was busy snoring because he went to bed and bumped his head. Said he couldn't get up in the morning. I looked over at his bed. Who's the babe? I ask him. He says her name's Collette. I guess she bumped her head, too, I say. Lots of that going around."

"What happened then?" I asked.

"The English dude went nuts, yelling about sinful behavior at the monastery. The French guy went nuts too, saying this Collette was two-timing him with Brother John the bell ringer. You would have thought it was the Hunchback of Notre Dame they were talking about. I was diplomatic. I said maybe Sister Collette should put her habit back on and split. It was better if everyone forgot what happened. If a story like that got out, well you know. I told them we could be paid professionals about it."

I looked at the Wolf.

He grinned back at me.

"Six hundred bucks," he said. "I forget where I got it. Can't remember a thing."

He handed three Benjamins over to me.

I was about to thank Wolfie when Beartina's voice came over the intercom.

"Your appointment with Patricia Duke. Shall I send her in?"

She entered in all her glory, exuding wealth by understating it. She wore the basic black dress with the pearls and spoke with her Kennedy accent. She shook hands with Wolfie and me and sat in the chair fronting my desk.

"I did exactly what you said to do, Bearstone," she said. "I went to the newspaper and told them the story about how Sonny Duke has been missing for seven days and that Samantha Greywitch has disappeared, too. The El Bruno Police have come up with nothing during that time, so it was time to move up to the top, the Bear With Us Detective Agency. I told them about Bearstone Blackie and Wolfie and how people should phone tips to you. Someone somewhere has to know something."

She was Sonny Duke's sister and had watched her playboy brother go from one sticky affair to another. He had accepted a dinner invitation from gourmet chef Samantha Greywitch, and now both had gone missing for a week.

She turned to the Wolf.

"I have to say; I don't trust that Greywitch woman. Maybe men are more susceptible to her charms, but not me. She's supposed to be a top notch chef."

"Yeah, that's why I hired her for my camp," Wolfie said. "That didn't work out too well. Ain't nothing but a pile of ashes where there once was a beautiful lodge. I don't know. Maybe that Gretel kid went too far in accusing Samantha Greywitch of cannibalism?"

Patricia tossed her head and smiled at Wolfie.

"Couple years back I hired her for a dinner party I was having," Patricia said. "I wanted it to be special. She said don't worry. I'll give you a jolly dish you could set before a king. She called it something like 'Sixpence and Rye.' I think she must have guzzled a fifth of the rye. Right after serving the salads, she brought out a large pie and cut it open. A couple dozen blackbirds staggered out of it. She had tried to bake them in the pie and get this: she actually expected them to sing after sitting in that hot pie. All they did was bleed and defecate all over my Queen Anne's lace table cloth."

"That's awful," Wolfie said. "I bet that was a shock."

"A large supply of Dom Perignon eased everyone's trauma," Patricia said.

"Is the newspaper going to put the reward information into the article?" I asked.

"Sure, " she said. "They'd better, they're owned by the Duke, Duke, Duke, Duke and Earl Trust. Speaking of finances, gentlemen here's five thousand dollars for you to get started. Keep me informed."

With that, she was up and out of our office.

The afternoon edition of the El Bruno Gazette was out an hour later. Our first real lead came minutes later when the phone rang.

"This that hotline about the missing Sonny Duke and that bimbo chef?"

"Yeah, Bearstone Blackie here. You got a tip we can use? You could get a thousand dollar reward if it bears out."

"The name's Tom Dorsey. I'm one of the guys who deliver the paper. Here's my tip: to go down by the station, early in the morning, see the little pufferbellies all in a row."

Click.

He was gone.

I played it back for Wolfie and Beartina.

"What'd he mean by that?" Beartina asked.

"What the hell's a pufferbelly?" Wolfie asked.

"If it's the police station, it must mean fat cops," Beartina said.

"Maybe it's the train station," I said. "Pufferbellies could mean fat train riders."

"Or fat trains," Beartina said. "Those old Thomas the Tank Engine locomotives could be pufferbellies."

We were up before dawn staking out the train station in El Bruno. Wolfie was on one end of the station platform, and I was on the other end. It was desolate, except for the dozen chocolate eclairs we brought from the Hungry Bear Donut Factory. Finally about 5:30 a small group of passengers arrived and waited for their train. In ten minutes the train arrived. They got on and left. The train was a streamlined diesel. No pufferbellies either on the train as passengers or the train itself. We waited until ten and left. Five trains had come, maybe a hundred passengers. No pufferbellies. We went back to the office.

The phone rang.

"It's Dorsey," the voice said. "Did you go down to the station, early in the morning, and see the little pufferbellies all in a row?"

"We just got back to the office," I said. "All we saw was the commuter train and a bunch of thin people."

"Ah, no," Dorsey said. "Wrong station. Pufferbelly Taco Station out at the El Bruno Marina."

Click.

He was gone again.

I called Patricia Duke.

"Bearstone, here. Does Sonny have a boat at the El Bruno Marina?"

"Yes, he does. It's called The Owl and the Pussycat."

"That's all I wanted to know," I said.

"Keep me informed, Bearstone," she said. "You know I'm concerned."

Pufferbelly Taco Station was a sailor's dream. It was also a taco lover's dream and a pufferbelly lover's dream. Customers sat under a large awning at the end of the main dock on old barstools around a circular counter. Your tacos were delivered by a small pufferbelly train. The menu was pretty simple, but all in Spanish so it took some doing for Wolfie and me to order our first six shrimp tacos, Tacos Camarones.

Before we sat for tacos, I walked the dock and found that The Owl and the Pussycat was not in its slip. I had a photo of Sonny that Patricia had given me. I introduced myself to the Pufferbelly Taco Station owner, Alfredo. Could I ask a few questions?

"Si, Senor Bearstone," Alfredo said.

I pointed to the photo of Sonny.

"This sailor went to sea." I motioned to the wide bay.

"Sea, si," Alfredo said. "See what he could see, si?"

"But all that he could see, see?" I showed him the photo of Samantha Greywitch.

"Ay Chihuahua! Buena Chica!" He grinned. "They go diving bottom of deep blue sea, see, si?"

"Diving?" I asked.

"Si, abalone."

"For baloney?" Wolfie asked.

"No baloney, abalone," Alfredo said.

Wolfie shrugged.

"Whatever."

"Sit down and enjoy the tacos," Alfredo said. "I make fresh coffee and tell you about how I collected all the pufferbellies."

It turned out Alfredo had been collecting pufferbellies since he was a little kid in Cabo San Lucas. He was president of the El Bruno chapter of Pufferbellies International. His shop sold Pufferbelly tee shirts in support of the upcoming Pufferbelly Fest to be held at the El Bruno International Amphitheater.

We had just finished putting on our new tee shirts and were into our second order of tacos when we heard a familiar voice behind us.

"Bearstone and Wolfie." It was Sonny. "You guys here for the great food?"

"Actually, we're here looking for you," I said. "Your sister got worried about you. She had the cops out looking for you. When they couldn't find you, she hired us. We got a hot tip that you might be here."

"Bet it was from Tom Dorsey," Sonny said. "He takes care of the boat, washes it down, keeps it waxed. He knew we were due back today."

I nodded.

"I hope Patricia paid you well. She can be kind of cheap," he said. "We just got in from diving for abalone. Took a week off and got to know each other really well. It turns out we have some common tastes we love to share with our friends."

Samantha Greywitch came up behind Wolfie and me and put an arm around each of us and squeezed off a big hug.

"You two are just so scrumptious, " she said. "I just can't wait to have you both for dinner."

The Tough Guys and the Beast Caper

It had been a busy morning at the Bear With Us Detective Agency. Wolfie and I had been coaching two over-the-hill actors on how to be tough guys in their next picture, a remake of the Maltese Falcon. How the two had gotten miscast as private eyes was one of those mysteries of Hollywood. Suffice it to say, both had iron-clad contracts and agents who knew where all the bodies were buried.

We won't use their real names here, but you can probably figure who's who without much trouble.

We'll call the bald one Delmer. We thought our course of action with him was to either shove a lollipop in his mug ala Kojak or give him a deep tan treatment and let him speak his lines in Ghetto Speak. Whichever way we went, "Who loves ya, Baby," always came out, "Who Wuvs you, Baby." Wolfie's suggestion of "Yo who loves you, baby? Brace yo'self fool!" just didn't help.

We tried another line: "All right, Louie, drop that gun. You ain't foolin' anyone." It came out, "Aw wight Wouie, Dwop that gun. You ain't foowin anyone."

The other guy was an even bigger disaster.

"Call me Sly," he said, except it came out "Thly."

I asked him where he was from.

"Kanthath Thity," he said. "Not Kanthath Thity Mithouri, but Kanthath Thity, Kanthath."

He was a strange-looking cat. He wore a black and white tux made out of some cheap fur. Every time he

63

spoke, he slobbered all over the front of it. I tried him on the line, "He certainly can't speak to you now, he's dead." After he stumbled through 'He thertaintly can't thpeak to you now, he'th dead,' he asked, "Couldn't I Jutht thay, 'Thufferin' Thuccotash,' inthtead?"

We gave them each a list of tough guy lines to practice until our next meeting, and they were on their way.

"Man, we should go do some Pufferbelly tacos at the marina," Wolfie said. "Must be lunchtime, no?"

I was about to agree when Beartina walked in.

"Some dude named Maurice just came by," she said. "He's got one wild story and money to pay someone who wants to listen. By the way, that Delmer guy's a real nice old fuddy-duddy. He signed an autograph for me and said we'd be invited to his movie's opening night."

"If he ever learns how to talk," Wolfie said.

"At least your face stays dry when he does," Beartina said. "Not like Sputter Puss."

Maurice came in and sat down in a chair in front of my desk. I said we wanted to hear his story. Figuring he had a French name, I offered everyone a croissant with brie on it from the Hungry Bear Donut Factory.

"Monsieur Bearstone, Monsieur Wolfie," he began. "I am an inventor who works for the benefit of our planet. I try to make machines that require little energy. I even ride my horse, Philippe, wherever I go when possible. I was traveling down to a fair to exhibit my latest wood cutting machine when I got lost in the vast forest. It was dark. I could hear voices that seemed to be on my tail as if they were chasing me. I didn't know what to do, but soon I saw the lights from a large mansion, and I headed there. I knocked on the large door, and it opened. I looked around for the person who opened the door and could find no one."

"The door maybe swung open with the force of your knock," Wolfie said.

64

"I thought the same thing," Maurice said. "But it turned out to be the candlestick."

"The candlestick?" I asked.

"You saying the candlestick opened the door for you?" Wolfie asked.

"I know it sounds strange, but it's the truth. A talking candlestick named Lumiere opened the door and invited me in. He told me he was under some spell just like Cogsworth the clock, Mrs. Potts the teapot and her son Chip the cup."

"Uh, they all talked to you, too?" Wolfie asked.

Maurice nodded.

"That bald guy and his friend in the cheap fur tuxedo that just left, they put you up to this?" Wolfie looked at Maurice.

"No, please it's what I saw, and now I'm worried about my daughter," Maurice said.

"Somebody cast a spell on her and turn her into an espresso machine?" I asked.

"Please, listen," Maurice said. "I know this sounds strange, but my daughter is out there, and I need your help. I have plenty of money. Here. There's five thousand dollars in the envelope. Please Monsieur Bearstone, Monsieur Wolfie."

I told him to go on with his tale. For five grand, I'd listen to trucks backfiring.

"Of course I was taken aback by what I encountered inside the mansion," Maurice went on. "In the confusion, I had forgotten to tie up my horse Philippe. He headed back to town without me. I didn't know what to do. Perhaps I could borrow another horse or even call a taxi to take me home, but then I turned and found myself looking into the face of a massive beast named Adam."

"Wait a minute," I said. "This Adam guy about seven feet tall, 300 pounds, built like a brick doo doo booth?"

Maurice nodded.

"He have pictures of himself all over the place? Dressed in sports uniforms?"

"Yes, how did you know?"

"It's Adam 'The Beast' Bearnoffsky," I said. "He's been on every bear athletic team. UCLA Bruins, Cal Golden Bears, Chicago Bears, Baylor Bears, Chicago Cubs, Boston Bruins, he's been kicked off of every one of them. Even the Fresno Grizzlies paid him to go away. The one thing he was always good at was taking the money and running off with some bimbo."

"So, how'd you get back to town?" Wolfie asked.

"I phoned my daughter, Belle and told her what had happened. My Philippe had run off. I was sitting with this Adam, and a talking candlestick was going to make me a snack. Belle hopped into her Mustang convertible and brought Philippe out to the Beast's mansion."

"Wait a second," Wolfie said. "I thought this Philippe was a horse. How'd she get him into the car?"

"Well, Philippe sometimes resembles a ten-speed bicycle. He won the Tour de France several years ago."

"What happened then?" I asked.

"The Beast looked at Belle and said, 'You are a Beauty!' Belle looked at him and said, 'I've heard that you can be a real naughty Beast.' Then she told me that Philippe had been getting fat and needed some exercise. If I rode him back to town and went to Gaston, it would help everything. She would stay and talk with the Beast. She wanted to learn more about this candlestick of his. Would it talk to her?"

"So, you rode back to town on Philippe the ten-speed horse and then what? She never showed up?" Wolfie rolled his eyes.

"As far as I know, three days later, she's still there," Maurice said. "And I have been trying to find her friend Gaston."

"You got the number of her cell phone?" I asked.

66

He wrote it down.

I buzzed Beartina to come in.

"Maurice needs to fill out contract papers," I said. "Can you take him to our lobby and give him package 28?"

Beartina nodded and smiled. Maurice followed her out, and she shut the door behind them.

"Package 28," Wolfie said. "Must be fifty pages long."

I dialed Belle's number.

When she answered, there was a lot of background noise before she spoke.

"No, you're such a Beast. You can't do that when I'm trying to talk on the phone. Wait until I'm off the phone. You know I'll like it better. Hello. This is Belle."

"Belle, this is Bearstone Blackie from the Bear With Us Detective Agency. Your dad, Maurice came in a few minutes ago to tell us he was worried about you. Are you okay?"

"Yes, I'm fine is Dad okay? He's supposed to have gone back to Gaston.

"Gaston? Yeah, he can't seem to find your friend Gaston.""

"Gaston Mental Health Clinic. He lives there. He gets confused when he doesn't take his meds. He starts thinking that Gaston is a person. Like he's some guy I'm involved with. When he doesn't medicate, he begins to hallucinate."

"Like seeing a talking candlestick?"

"Yeah, it doesn't talk, Bearstone. It has other talents." She giggled.

"Your dad came in and offered us five thousand dollars to make sure that you were all right. He said he was on his way to show off his newly invented woodcutter machine when he happened upon Adam's place."

"Bearstone, I'm so sorry this has happened," she said. "Dad keeps thinking that a simple hand saw is something he's just invented. If you look in the envelope, you'll see that it's all Monopoly money."

Sure enough, it was.

"Are you sure that you're okay out there with Adam?"

"We're only two miles from town. Yes, I'm having a very good time. The place is so well decorated with designer furniture and designer drugs. I mean designer rugs. Adam is a prince, and he's treating me like a princess. Listen, how about taking Dad over to Gaston for me? Would five hundred bucks do it?"

I told her it would.

"Wait, don't hang up." She said. "Adam wants to talk to you."

"Bearstone, can you and the Wolf bring your ladies to a barbecue fundraiser I'm having for Mayor Bear Nays re-election this Saturday around two? The Ribs & Pepper Bistro is catering. Old King Cole and Fiddlers Three will play Merry Old Soul music. Should be a fun crowd."

I told him we'd come. He gave directions. Part of the five hundred we'd get for delivering Maurice back to the laughing academy would end up in the Mayor Nays campaign fund.

Luckily, Philippe the ten-speed bicycle didn't turn into Philippe the horse in the trunk of my car as we drove Maurice to the Gaston Mental Health Clinic.

We checked them both in and headed for lunch.

"You know what I'm wondering?" Wolfie grinned.

"What's that?"

"Which one of our tough guy actors is going to murder the last line of the Maltese Falcon? Probably too much work to get Baldy to say, 'Yo da shit dat dreams is made o'."

"Yeah," I said. " 'The thtuff that dreamth are made of,' might be the best that we can do."

68

The Honeymoon Caper

It was a quiet morning at the Bear With Us Detective Agency. Wolfie and I were enjoying lemon cannoli from the Hungry Bear Donut Factory. We had root beers from the Thirsty Dragon Root Beer Factory and were reading the latest stories from two of our favorite sources, the National Inquisitor, and the El Bruno Gazette.

"Here's one from the El Bruno fish wrapper," Wolfie said. "Pervert Seized While Terrorizing Town."

"Shocking," I said. "Read on."

"Wee Willie Winkie ran through the town, upstairs and downstairs in his nightgown, rapping at the windows, crying through the lock and asking if kids were in bed because it was eight o'clock."

"You sure it's Winkie and not Wilkin? The cop story in the Inquisitor says that Willy Wilkin kissed the maids a milking and with his merry daffing he set them all a-laughing."

"What's that mean?" Wolfie asked. "He's got a merry daffing? What's it do, tell jokes? Who writes this garbage?"

"Wow, look at this." I turned the front page of the Inquisitor toward Wolfie. The headline screamed, "International Serial Killer Suspects at Large, Hundreds of Victims."

"Read that one to me," Wolfie said.

I read it:

Surete Internationale Director Jacques Clouseau announced a worldwide manhunt for three suspects. Clouseau alleges the three were behind hundreds of murders in Europe and the United States. Authorities are searching for Jessica Fletcher of Cabot Cove, Maine, Jane Marple of St. Mary Mead, England, and Hercule Poirot of Belgium.

"These are people who wrote the book on murders and then went and pulled them off," Clouseau said. "They were clever as minkies in every case, pretending to solve each case, while skillfully blaming innocent people for their dastardly crimes. Fletcher alone is responsible for over 260 deaths. Some of her victims received a bimp on the head by a blunt object. Her series 'Murder, She Wrote' should be retitled 'Murder, She Wrought.' Marple and Poirot are cut out of the same ugly cloth, posing as innocents while doing their dastardly deeds."

"Wow," Wolfie said.
"Could be something to that," I said. "Think about it. Every time one of them showed up somewhere, some poor bugger died."
Wolfie nodded.

We sipped our root beers and crunched another cannoli.

"Here's one about that local gang of toughs, the Simple Simons," Wolfie said. "Seems they met a pie man heading to the fair. One of the toughs says to the guy, 'we want to taste your ware.' The pie man ain't no fool. He says, 'show me the money.' The toughs say, 'we ain't got any.' They're about to grab the goods when Mr. Pie Man introduces the boys to Mr. Smith and Mr. Wesson. Couple Simple Simons won't be tasting pie unless they're serving it in the after-life. El Bruno's finest showed up after the gunplay and got the pie man for carrying without a permit."

I was about to read another story when Beartina walked in from our outer office.

"You wouldn't believe the two foul balls that want to see you two," she said. "Couple old dudes who still think they got it. Can't find their young wives. A blowhard and a dummy."

"Just our types," Wolfie said. "Send them in."

They came in. I motioned for them to sit down in the chairs in front of my desk.

"I'm Bearstone Blackie, and that's my partner Wolfram T. Wolf over on our designer Naugahyde sofa."

"Call me Ralph," the fat guy said. He wore a jacket that said Gotham Bus Company in lettering above the front pocket.

The thin guy wore an open vest, a white tee shirt, and a pork pie hat.

"Norton," the thin guy said. "Or call me Ed. Just don't call me late to dinner."

He laughed and slapped Ralph on the arm. Ralph frowned at Norton.

"We're out here from New York on our honeymoon," Ralph said.

"Congratulations," I said. "You two look like you're made for each other."

"No, not us," Ralph said. "I mean it's us, but not to each other, couple of good looking women. We came here to see some of your sights, like the ketchup factory and the Hungry Bear Donut Factory."

"Worth the trip in itself," I said.

"I should give you a retainer," Ralph said. "Would three thousand be about right?"

I nodded, biting my lip to keep from smiling.

He counted out thirty Ben Franklins and slid them toward me.

"We, uh, got a little problem," Ralph said. "We're married to a couple of real lookers and, well, we gave the girls enough dough to choke a couple of horses so they could go shopping. Well, they haven't been back."

He wiped sweat from his brow.

"How long they been gone?" Wolfie asked.

"Uh, it's the third day," Norton said. "Sheesh, they must be having a great time, eh Ralphie Boy?"

Ralphie Boy rolled his eyes.

"How much money did you give them?" I asked.

"Fifty thousand each," Norton said. "They needed it to buy some clothes. They're new to this country, and we're loaded, so why not?"

"That's right," Ralphie Boy said. "We made big money later in life, and now we want to enjoy it. My first wife, Alice. What a turkey. She said I'd never get anywhere driving a bus."

"Hey you got to Manhattan and Brooklyn," Norton said. "You even got to Rikers after you popped her one."

Norton laughed.

"Yeah, I kept warning her," Ralph said. "Finally did it. Pow, right in the kisser."

"And she hit him right back, broke his nose." Norton laughed and slapped the desk.

"Never mind that," Ralph said. "Your marriage to Trixie was no picnic."

"He's right," Norton said. "Trixie, my first old lady. Same thing. She kept harping, 'You know a lot about the sewers and water treatment plants, but what good will that do you, Ed?' Hah, that's exactly how Ralph and I struck it rich. I'm glad she divorced me."

Wolfie covered a laugh and shook his head at the two characters.

"So you struck it rich driving a bus and knowing about sewers and underground water pipes in New York?" I asked.

72

Ralph looked over at Norton and winked.

"Should we tell him, Pal o' mine?"

"Why not? We're rollin' in it, Ralph. We don't need to work another day in our lives."

"Okay," Ralph leaned forward and leaned on the desk.

"We ran into a guy who needed help educating engineering students about how a complicated city like New York works with all its electric, sewers, water and gas lines. Well, we knew a lot of that. Norton had the info, and I had the bus. So we'd take these students on a tour of all the facilities that keep New York working."

"Yeah," Norton said. "This guy who ran the program had a big grant, and he said he'd give us each a couple million to take these minority college kids from Middle-Eastern States on our tours. You know a lot of people from Delaware and Maryland don't know New York. Hell, these kids could barely understand English. So, that's what we did. That's how we can afford our new Russian wives."

"Russian wives?" I asked.

"We just came back from Moscow a week ago," Ralph said. "They got hundreds of women over there dying to meet wealthy American men."

"The Kalashnikov sisters," Norton said. "Va va va voom. I told Ralph, hey, I'll take the redhead or the blonde. Either way."

"Yeah," Ralph said. "That's what he said, but I'm the brains between the two of us. I knew that he knew that I knew that he wanted the redhead. So, I said to him, go ahead and take her. If it don't work out, we'll get you one that does."

He and Norton started laughing. Ralph broke into a coughing fit.

"Too many Havanas," Ralph said.

Wolfie stared at me and shook his head.

"So, Ralph," I said. "You been to the cops with this problem of yours?"

"No, we haven't." He looked down at the floor and then up at me. "You start telling the cops about handing out fifty thousand dollars to your Russian wives, and they think you're peddling drugs or weapons. All we did was run a tour bus for engineering students."

"Yeah, all we got left to do is deliver their luggage to the airport in our bus," Norton said. "Don't even have to unload it. Just leave the bus in the departure drop-off lane and grab a cab. Hit a call button on a cell phone to tell them where we left it. Pretty snazzy deal, eh?"

I told them to wait out in the front office while Wolfie and I talked over their case. Wolfie grabbed one of the chairs and slid it close to me.

"I hope you got Homeland Security on speed dial," he said.

The FBI agents who arrived minutes after our call were happy to be involved in a slam-dunk case that could lead to busting up a terrorist cell.

"I've been going nuts looking at emails," Agent Magda Prickly said. "This case is great. I don't think these guys even know what email is."

Out in the front office, I could hear Prickly's partner, Agent Andover Stickly interviewing Ralphie Boy and Norton. The three sat around a table that held a recorder.

"What do you think you were involved in?" Stickly asked.

"Just helping engineering students and their teacher," Norton said. "Mr. Kiter. Think his first name was Al? Right Ralph? We were working for Al Kiter. Right Ralph?"

Ralph's eyes bulged out as he tried to stand and catch his breath.

All he could manage before fainting was, "Homina, homina, homina."

74

The Clown Caper

It was morning coffee and bagel time at the Bear With Us Detective Agency. My partner, Wolfram T. "Wolfie" Wolf and I were watching one of our training videos, attempting to keep up with latest crime-fighting techniques in a town where anything could happen, and it unusually did. I'm private eye Bearstone Blackie. I fight crime.

On the screen, two detectives were interrogating a suspect in a police lockup:

"So where have you been, Billy Boy, Billy Boy?" First Detective asked.

"Yeah where have you been, Charmin Billy?" Second Detective asked. "Charmin? They call you that because they think you're toilet paper? Something you wipe your butt on? Is that what they think of you out on the street?"

"No, it's Charming, not Charmin," Billy folded his arms and stared at the tabletop.

"Yeah," First Detective said. "On his sheet, it says 'Charming comma Billy.' You got a middle name of 'Prince?' Just like a dog. Here Prince. That you, Prince Charming? So where you been Billy Boy?"

"Lay off," Billy said. "I been to see my wife, she's the joy of my life."

"Yeah, but she's a young thing and can't leave her mother, but that didn't stop you did it?" Second Detective slammed his fist down on the table.

"She bade me to come in," Billy mumbled

"Billy Boy, Billy Boy," First Detective said. "Cut the crap. She's under age. So you went in. Now you're in the house, and you don't care. You're just after the daughter."

"You like 'em real young, don't you Billy Boy?" Second Detective lit a cigarette and blew the smoke into Billy's face.

"You want to start telling us about the cherry pie, Billy Boy?" First Detective leaned into Billy's face. "You get out front on this and maybe it will go easier on you."

"Are you two just gonna loaf around all morning watching stupid cop shows?" Beartina asked. She walked into my office and clicked off the TV. "I just got back from the bank. There are people waiting to see you two in our lobby."

"What's up?" I asked.

"Guess you didn't see the morning El Bruno Gazette?"

She tossed the paper on my desk. The headline read; "Clown Goes Missing, Possible Foul Play Suspected."

"Who's out in the lobby?" I asked. "Not the clown?"

"No, the circus owners."

"Send them in."

Two over-weight women wearing lion tamer outfits complete with riding crops walked in.

"You must be Bearstone," the red-headed woman said. "And this guy over here must be Wolfie."

"You got that one right, Red," I said. "Who are you and who's your friend?"

They both sat down in chairs facing my desk. Red slapped the side of my desk with her riding crop. I could see Wolfie sitting on our Naugahyde sofa, smiling as he waited for things to develop.

"Dina and Dinah Dingling, from Dingling Sisters, Bearnum and Bear Lee Circus," Red said. "Dinah's the cheap black dye job. I'm the expensive scarlet tint job from Mister Jister's Salon down in Jeopardy. We played there all last week, well at least until the clown disappeared. That pretty much shut things down. He was headed up here. Said he'd meet us out at the circus grounds, but it's been two days and no clown."

"I can't help but notice how you're dressed," I said. "You weren't using your riding crops on the clown, were you?"

"No," Dina said. "Fact is, you can't use whips on anything these days. We had to get rid of the elephants, the cats, the gorilla. Now, we're strictly acrobats, ponies, wire walkers and the clown, Boozo by name. He does magic tricks and comedy bits. He's been having troubles lately."

"What kind of troubles?" I asked. "He hitting the sauce? Losing on the ponies? Got some dame after him?"

"No, not like that," Dina said. "He gets into fights with people. Has to run for his life. It's that evil clown thing going around. What they call it, Dinah?"

"Sinister Clown," Dinah rasped. If anyone had been hitting the sauce, it was Dinah, whose voice was like a Mynah.

"People see him outside the circus tent, and they think he's some kinda Stephen King character, like he's gonna kill someone," Dina said. "Last I heard from him, he was coming to El Bruno to get help from some doctor. He figured maybe he was sending out some hostility to people."

"One of those moon worshipping holistic creeps, that's who he was going to see," Dinah said. "Dr. Gecko, like that reptile in those goofy insurance commercials."

"Except we looked all over Hell for a Doctor Gecko and we can't find him," Dina said. "Boozo has disappeared and this Gecko guy, well, I just don't know. That's why we're here. Maybe you can help."

I told her we'd look for the clown. I had a few ideas. She dropped a grand on the desk, told us they were staying in their motorhomes out at the circus grounds and the two of them left.

"Mama, I hope them's not circus tickets," Wolfie said. "Nothin' like greenback hundreds."

I had an idea of who they were looking for. There was a Doctor Shekkle who ran a feel good/fat farm out near Limbo. He was one of those guys who spoke of everyone's yin and yang personalities. If you had too much yin, you needed more yang. Shekkle sold supplements that might or might not make that balance happen. He also sold books and videos that instructed the customer on how to turn everything into a healthy, wealthy, sexy life that others could only dream about. His slogan was, "If you can dream it, you can scheme it."

Wolfie and I had last met Shekkle at a fundraiser for Mayor Bear Nays re-election. Shekkle thought the mayor was a balanced yin-yang person whereas whenever Shekkle got near the Wolf and me, he'd say something like, "Too much yang, hot liver."

The Wolf would reply, "Fry it with bacon and onions and I'll eat all the hot liver you can dish."

We pulled up to the main building at Shekkle's place. There was a crowd of people on the lawn doing tai chi. I didn't see a clown among them. We went inside.

"Can I help you, sir?" The receptionist was dressed in what looked like a potato sack with epaulets on it.

"Bearstone Blackie and Mr. Wolf to see Dr. Shekkle."

"Are you a patient, sir?"

I couldn't reply. Shekkle was already at the desk.

"Bearstone, Wolfie, why am I being so honored?"

"We're looking for some clown named Boozo. His employers think he might have come here for treatment. They're worried about him."

"Follow me," Shekkle said. "There's nothing to worry about. There's a rampant case of clown phobia taking the country by storm, however. Boozo and I are working on ways to disarm the hysteria."

We came to a room that was padded inside. Was it a cell? Maybe. A guy in a clown suit sat on one of the built-in bunks.

"Boozo?"I asked.

"You're not here to hit me, are you?" he asked.

"No, we're here to see if you're okay. The Dingling sisters have hired us to see that you're safe."

"You boys are here just in time to see our latest treatment," Dr. Shekkle said. "I've prepared this elixir that can reverse the polarity of an overloaded yin yang situation. It replaces aggression with understanding and meekness with confidence. It supplies what's missing in the personality."

"You mean the clown here is going to drink this, and everything will be okay?" Wolfie asked. "Nobody going to chase him to beat him up?"

"Yes," Shekkle said. "Remember. Perception is reality. No harm will come. Don't believe me? Watch, I'll drink it."

Shekkle drained the glass of green smoking liquid and sat down on the bunk opposite Boozo. He was quiet for a minute.

We waited.

Shekkle's face seemed different.

He leaned forward and rasped out a word: "Clown!"

He looked at Wolfie and then me.

"Wolfie and Bearstone," he rasped again. "Don't any of you have any decent clothes to wear? Is this a tailor's nightmare? You three are pathetic."

"Yeah?" Wolfie said. "Where you get off? Who you think you are?"

"I'm Mr. Snide and you three are pathetic."

"What happened to Dr. Shekkle?" I asked.

"Shekkle's a phony. He puts out all that yin yang horseshit. I'm the real personality. Shekkle feeds everyone a bunch of crap about the vegan diet, safe sex, drug-free lifestyle and guess what? After hours, I take over. The cocktails flow down at the Boom Boom Room. You ought to see some of the wild babes that hang around there."

Boozo grabbed a towel off the bed and started to wipe the clown makeup off his face. He kicked off the over-sized shoes and was soon down to his tee shirt and shorts.

"I've had it," Boozo said. "No more of this clown crap. No more of this yin yang crap. Can you boys give me a ride to my trailer at the circus?"

"Sure enough," I said.

Shekkle/Snide sat still on the bed.

He looked like he was coming out of a trance.

He was back to being Shekkle.

"You boys taking off with Boozo?"

"Yeah, he's got it all thought out," Wolfie said.

"Great, another patient cured," Shekkle said.

We drove toward the circus grounds with Boozo. He seemed happy to be out of the clown suit.

"I can't thank you guys enough," he said. "Can you do me one more favor? I'd like to change clothes and if it isn't asking too much, could you drop me at the Boom Boom Room?"

The Comic Strip Caper

It was a slow morning at the Bear With Us Detective Agency. My partner Wolfie and I were going through old cases in our files.

"Remember that one with the guy looking for that sea captain?" Wolfie asked. "Hawkins? Wasn't he here about a month ago?"

"Yeah, Jim Hawkins." I took a bite of my onion bagel with lox from the Hungry Bear Donut Factory. "He's another one of those lost buried treasure hunter guys. El Bruno's a seaport. We get a lot of that going on."

"I hear you," Wolfie said. "He came in here looking for some pirate. Like we got a file drawer full of pirates. What'd he think this is Zanzibar?"

"So, we sent him to the Muffin Man down on Drury Lane," I said. "A dive like that would be a good place to start. That guy Tony Coloratura who hangs out down there knows a lot of sailors. They say he Shanghais some of them. If Hawkins had given us any money out front, we would have gone with. I thought he was just a pain in the butt."

"Real pain in the butt," Wolfie said. "He brought back that old guy with a hook for a hand and wanted us to find out where he had hidden the treasure. Too much rum and cola, if you ask me."

"Yeah, how do you confuse Captain Hook with Long John Silver? Hook stood there mumbling about some crocodile with a ticking clock in its stomach coming after him. Imagine that, a crocodile in El Bruno?"

"The crocodile would have made a better client than Hawkins," Wolfie said. "All those guys are looking for is something for nothing. They remind me of one of my nephews, Chiseler D. Wolf. First time I shook hands with him, I knew he was a crook."

"How so?"

"I went to reach for my wallet in my jacket pocket. His hand was already there grabbing for it. Said he was collecting unique leather goods."

Beartina walked into the office and closed the door behind her.

"Couple upset women waiting to see you guys," she said. "They look familiar. I think they were in show biz back in the day."

"Send them in," I said.

They came in and sat down next to each other in chairs facing my desk.

Both were well-dressed and gave off that "real money can buy good facelift" look. I guessed both were in their sixties, maybe older. The more round-faced of the two spoke first.

"I'm Nancy Ritz, Mr. Bearstone. Am I right that this is the Wolf?" She pointed at our Naugahyde sofa where the Wolf sat.

I nodded.

"We're on the run from a couple abusive husbands," she said. "It's not like a Thelma and Louise thing, but it could get that way. We've both been beaten and cheated out of our hard-earned money. Not all of it, to be sure, but enough to try to keep away from the two losers we happened to marry."

"And you are?" I asked, pointing my face toward the thinner faced of the two.

"Lulu Tompkins," she said. There were tears in her eyes. "I've been using the name Little as of late. I really don't want anything to do with Tubby, or whatever he's calling himself these days."

Their stories unfolded. Both women had been big stars in syndicated features in newspapers all over the world. Each had married their co-stars. Nancy had married a bum from the slummier part of town who went by the name Sluggo Smith. Lulu picked someone from the same school she attended. His name was Tompkins. Tubby Tompkins. For a while things were fine, but then the men started to see that the women were the real stars and the two men just a couple character actors who happened into a pot of gold by marrying their wives.

"Sluggo Smith thought he was a tough guy from a rough part of town," Nancy said. "The only one he could beat up was me after he had a snoot full. I can't tell you how many times I called the cops on him. But the cops are worthless. I decided to run away with Lulu, here. We met on one of those comic convention tours."

Lulu picked up the story.

"Being around Tubby was a trip. He had his own strip for a couple try-outs, but they both went nowhere. He started hitting the sauce hard. Sometimes when he was sober enough, he'd do a bit part in my strip, but it was never what you'd call quality work. Everybody involved in the production thought he was a loser. He liked belonging to 'white men, only' clubs, started doing that as a kid. When his strip folded, he got involved in one of those tribute bands as a singer. It was a takeoff on Culture Club. He called himself Boy Gorge. Dressing up in the draggy costume almost led him to a nervous breakdown. He found it hard to give up his little sailor's hat. He still wears it."

I looked at both of them. They had been big stars, and now they were on the run from a couple of punks.

"What can we do for you?" I asked.

"For starters, Mr. Bearstone," Lulu said, "We wanted to beat them here to you. They said they were going to hire you to find us. We want to be your clients, denying them the possibility of using your services. Can you help us there?"

"Say we do that," Wolfie said. "They still are going to come after you. You say the cops are no help? What if we can somehow send them off on a wild goose chase?"

"Anything like that would help," Nancy said.

"And you think they're on your tail?" I asked.

"They knew we were coming out here for a comic convention," Lulu said. "We're staying at the El Bruno Biltmore, registered under the name Blondie and Cookie Bumstead."

"Why them?" Wolfie asked.

"Listen, Honey," Nancy said. "I could tell you stories about what that poor family went through with Mr. Drugwood. None of it's very pretty. Blondie heard we were in trouble and she wanted to help."

I told the two women to head back to their hotel. I'd keep them posted after I saw the two husbands.

Wolfie and I returned from lunch to find Sluggo and Tubby waiting for us. I motioned for them to come into the office and sit where their estranged spouses had sat only two hours before.

Tubby spoke first. He had one of those phony "I've been to Oxford voices."

"Mr. Bearstone, we have heard a great deal about you and the Wolf, and we think you might be just right for finding our wives. Both of them are being treated for schizophrenic behavior and have escaped from the institution where they were staying. We need your help to find them."

He described who they were and how both wives had become famous due to the coaching of their talented husbands.

"We're afraid they might hurt themselves," Sluggo said. "They've given themselves black eyes and bloody noses in the past." Sluggo had a voice like Peter Lorre on gravel.

Tubby shoved a couple of pictures of Nancy and Lulu across the desk toward me.

"Good looking dames," I said. "Too bad they're nutso. Must be rough on you guys."

"And how, " Tubby said. "Neither of us have had any action on that front in a while."

I looked at the two losers and made my play.

"You're looking at a grand to get us going," I said. "We should have satisfaction in a day or two. Can you wait that long?"

"Sure," Tubby said. "Say, you don't know anywhere around here where a couple guys like us can get some action, do you?"

"Oh, man," Wolfie said. "You came to the right wolf. I'm gonna call you a cab right now. Take you down to the Muffin Man Bar. You're gonna want to talk to Tony when you get there."

They dropped a grand on my desk and headed out the door with Wolfie who put them in the cab. He came back into the office and found Beartina and me laughing.

"Why so happy?" he asked. "Beartina's been listening to us?"

"I just got off the phone with your Mary," Beartina said. "She's happy that you two are taking us out tonight with that money you just squeezed out of those two."

"Freshly squozen and not frozen," I said. "And what did Tony have to say to the Wolf?"

"Tony said he needed a couple of tough guys like Sluggo and Tubby to paint a garbage scow while it sails to Somalia," Wolfie said. "I told Tony that one of the guys I was sending even had a sailor's hat. 'Hope he's not in a hurry,' Tony said. 'Could take three or four years at sea to get there.'"

The Christmas, Carol Caper

It was a quiet December morning at the Bear With Us Detective Agency. My partner Wolfie and I were watching detective training videos to keep us sharp in our profession. Just as Columbo was about to put the screws to Wayne Newton, we were interrupted by holiday commercial messages:

"That itsy bitsy spider won't climb up a badly damaged, unsightly water spout and Santa Claus won't like it either. Call Crankhead Plumbing and Roofing to get your home ready for holiday visitors…"

And:

"You can ride a cock horse to Branbury Cross Music to see a fine lady upon a white horse, but rings on her fingers and bells on her toes? No, Man. Buy her a Fender, and she'll have sizzling music wherever she goes…"

And:

"Motor Mouth Mike here for Princess and the Pea Mattress Company. Hey, have we got a holiday sale going on in our showrooms. Get our Chanukah/Christmas/Kwanza/New Years special delivered tonight to your castle…"

"You boys better shut that thing off." It was Beartina, receptionist, office manager, bookkeeper, and love of my life. "A paying customer is waiting to see you two. Her name's Carol Christmas."

"Christmas gets here sooner every year," Wolfie said.

She came in and sat down after being introduced to Wolfie and me. She was a well-dressed woman in her thirties. Everything about her said business with a capital B. If you said Silicon Valley executive, she'd fit the bill.

"I've heard a lot about you guys and never thought that I'd be needing you," she said. "You've probably heard of me."

"Mortgages, tech investments, initial public offerings," Wolfie said. "You did right by your customers during the Crash. Your partner Jacob Marley took off for the islands with whatever he could grab."

"Jake Marley," she said. "That's why I'm here. He showed up at my house late last night. I thought he was dead until he rang my bell. I heard he had gotten involved in drug-running in Colombia and fell in with the wrong crowd."

I nodded.

"Didn't they call you 'The Scrooge' at one time?" Wolfie asked.

"Yeah, some of my employees called me that during the crash of '08," she said. "I'm kind of proud of being called 'The Scrooge.' I was adamant that no one got bonuses on our staff until all our customers were treated fairly. When Marley took off with what he could grab, that made it doubly hard. I ended up selling a large tract of land out in the Valley to make it through the crisis."

"So what does Marley want?" I slid the tray of lemon-flavored cannoli toward her.

"Wow, the cannoli treatment," she said. "I've heard about this. A wonderful way to treat clients."

She took a cannoli and a napkin.

"Our pleasure," I said. "Tell us about Marley."

"He's always been after me. He's a real sexual predator, fancies himself as a ladies man. He got into all that Santeria stuff down in the islands. He's bringing over someone named Mama Cubana, a practitioner to make me see three apparitions tonight. I want you guys to be there. I don't trust him."

"What about the cops?" I asked.

"Useless, if not worse," she said. "Some said that Marley got away so easily when the market crashed because he had some law enforcement help in leaving the country."

"Think he has any of them helping him now?" I asked.

"Yeah, they'll probably make sure he gets out of the country."

"So, you think he's going to hit you up for some more money?" Wolfie asked.

"Yeah, he'd want me to fall in love with him and run off with some more of other people's money."

"We'll be happy to have you as a client," I said.

Wolfie and I arrived at the Christmas house shortly before midnight. A maid met us at the door and brought us in. A round table was set with chairs around it in the main parlor. Carol Christmas was already at the table, nervously rubbing her hands. Several minutes later, Marley arrived with the Santeria practitioner, a dark-skinned woman with long wild hair and a dress that flowed to the floor.

"Who are these two mugs?" Marley asked. He was a greasy-looking blowhard in a flashy suit that said bordello operator.

"Bearstone Blackie and my associate, The Wolf," I said. "We're here to make sure that Mama Cubana over here shuffles the deck right."

"She doesn't use a deck," Marley said. He sat down next to her and slapped her arm. "Get to work. Do your thing."

She took a dead chicken out of her sack and squeezed some blood out of it onto some coins in a small dish. She took out a dollar bill and set it on fire and put it in the dish with the coins and the chicken blood. Then she took out a candle and lit it, placing it in the dish.

"You must turn off the lights," she cackled. "You want to see the visions."

The maid came in and turned off the overhead chandelier.

Wolfie sat on one side of Carol. I sat on the other.

"We supposed to hold hands?" Carol asked.

"No need," Marley said.

"We first bring to life the spirit of the Christmas past," Mama Cubana cackled.

"Uh, is that Christmas past as in the holiday or as in Carol Christmas?" Wolfie asked.

"Don't try to break the spell with questions," Mama Cubana said. "I'm getting an image. We have a presence about to make itself known to us."

Something under the table rumbled. A deep voice groaned and a vapor-like vision formed above the table.

"Tell us who you are," Mama Cubana said. "Are you the spirit of Christmas Past?"

"I am," groaned the voice. "I remember a sad Carol Christmas one Christmas when she was stuck at school without her relatives to share the holidays with."

"When was this?" Carol asked.

"Your senior year at the University of Hawaii," the voice groaned.

"You must have had the wrong Carol Christmas," Carol said. "I was seeing a great guy. We went surfing every day. We went to the symphony, saw plays and heard some dynamite blues."

"But, you had no relatives with you," the voice insisted.

"Yeah, not until Aunt Mildred arrived and wanted me to take her to the Jehovah's Wit-less meetings. That's when things got sad."

"Oh, oh, I fear I'm losing my energy," the voice said. "I'm fading back into the ether world. I've delivered my message."

"So, what's that supposed to mean?" Carol asked.

"It means you need to see things my way," Marley said. "You're too focused on being a goody-two-shoes. Look at me. When the going got rough, I got going, south of the old border. You want me to sing the rum and Coca-Cola song. Hell, I could have us all dancing around this table."

Mama Cubana raised her hand.

"I am feeling another presence. Yes, it is the presence of Christmas present."

"Uh, you want to hold off with your rap a second?" Wolfie asked. "Are you talking about Christmas presents, as in gifts, or do I have to be worried about some cut-rate voice coming out of the woodwork at us as in presence?"

"You will find out Mr. Wolfie," Mama Cubana said. "The voice will report what is going on at the house of Carol's employee Mr. Bob Catshit on Christmas morning."

"Uh, that's Cratchit," Carol said. "Not Catshit."

"What does it matter?" Marley asked. "Another of Carol's nose to the grindstone employees."

A rumble came from under the table, and a shaking high-pitched voice began speaking. A weaker looking spirit hovered above the table.

"Such a terrible time at the Catshit house. Bob has no work, no job. Carol has told him to be gone. Bob's son Tiny Tim sits in a corner, crippled, wearing braces on his legs and casts on his wrists of blackened cloth. The house will soon be in mourning over a future tragedy."

"Boy, you almost got that one right," Carol said. "Bob has no work for the next three weeks. He and his family are spending that time at my condo on Maui. Tim has the pads on his legs and arms to protect himself while he competes in the skateboard championships Christmas week. The only mourning over a coming tragedy is Bob's insistence on betting on the Chicago Bears."

"Good old Carol," Marley said. "Always trying to paint a rosy picture out of misery. Tell the truth. When I took off with the loot didn't you think about finding fun-loving Jake down in the islands so the two of us could have a life together? I mean I always saw you giving me the eye."

"Maybe the evil eye," Carol said.

"Ah, playing hard to get," Marley said. "I love it when I have to make a conquest in the art of love."

"You got another spook showing up?" Wolfie asked. "Or is Marley's speech the last one?"

"We have the spirit of Christmas yet to come," Mama Cubana said. "A look into the future. Perhaps we should all be afraid."

"Yeah, the way the election turned out," Wolfie said.

"Please, I am trying to contact a presence from the ether world," Mama Cubana said. "He will tell us about the sadness yet to come in the life of Carol Christmas and how it can be prevented by giving in to Mr. Marley's wishes and becoming his lover."

"He would tell you that, but unfortunately we caught him in the driveway trying to make off with some jewelry and silver service," a voice said from under the table.

"Who is that?" Mama Cubana shrieked. "Is it a real presence? Forgive me, Spirit. I meant no harm, Spirit. Just having fun with a few people. Christmas party, yeah?"

FBI Agent Magda Prickly stepped into the room. Two agents behind her had the maid and a sullen-looking man in handcuffs.

"We figured out their little scheme here, thanks to Wolfie and Bearstone," Prickly said. "There's a reward out for Marley and his crew. They're all flight risks."

Agent Andover Stickly stepped over to Marley and cuffed him.

"They were using a cheap wireless mike and a small amplifier under the table," Stickly said. "There's a cheap hologram device mounted up on the wall supplying the shaky ghost above the table trick. They probably put it there when you went to visit Bearstone and Wolfie. The maid let them in. She's Marley's niece, in case you didn't know."

Wolfie and I watched with Carol as Marley and his cohorts were placed into FBI cruisers.

"You two guys are fantastic," Carol said. "You knew just what to do, who to contact. Be sure to send me your bill. Oh, something else. I mentioned my condo on Maui?"

We nodded.

"Well, I have an even better one on the Big Island," she said. "Why don't you and your ladies take it for a month? You can probably use the time to relax, maybe catch some fish."

"Wow," I said.

"This really is a Merry Christmas," the Wolf said.

"Actually, Merry is my sister," Carol said.

The Legends and Voices Caper

It was a typical morning at the Bear With Us Detective Agency. My partner Wolfie and I were involved in a taste test involving chocolate cannoli versus the mango-flavored variety while we watched a cultural offering on history, religion, and pest control.

It was the Harry Stringer Show.

Harry's guests represented three of the cultural and religious organizations in town. They were discussing the upcoming parade celebrating diversity in El Bruno. It was called "Legendary Truths on Parade."

"Nigel Mountbatten represents the St. George Association of Knights," Harry Stringer said. "Tell us, Nigel, will you be displaying the dragon that St. George reputedly slew?"

"Reputedly? My arse," Nigel said. "We've got a mock up of the ancient beast and he'll stretch out for sixty feet down Main Street. Our regal St. George is twelve feet high. Much better than what any of these other blighters on your show have to offer."

Harry's audience roared to life. Shouts came from the seats.

"Jolly good, Nigel."

"I say, good show, old boy."

Now the camera was on a red-nosed man in a green suit.

"What about that, Seamus O' Rourke?" Harry asked. "You represent the St. Patrick Marchers. What will your group be doing? Will it be better than the St. George offering?"

"Hah, we'll always be better than what some pathetic limey comes up with," Seamus said. "We'll be having a seventy-foot snake being driven out of Ireland by a fifteen foot St. Patrick and we'll be handing out shamrocks to viewers in the crowd."

Harry's audience cheered again, louder.

"Up the IRA."

"Sinn Fein."

"Erin go bragh."

"A third group in the parade is the Iron Cross Pied Piper of Hamelin Society, celebrating a legendary hero from beyond the Rhine," Harry said. "Here with us today is Horst Gruber to describe his group's entry."

Horst stood, flashing his monocle at the camera.

"As you know, Harry," Horst began, "We have the best entry, every time. We have a twenty foot tall Pied Piper driving an eighty-foot long rat out of Hamelin. The Piper will be playing songs based on where he's taking all the rats to their new festering garbage dumps."

"What songs?" Harry asked.

"We're having him play 'My Wild Irish Rose' and 'God Save the Queen.'"

Harry's audience roared again. Someone threw a chair toward the stage. Nigel Mountbatten leaped at Horst Gruber.

"Bloody fascist," Nigel yelled, swinging his fists.

The audience began fighting among themselves. Ushers jumped into the melee.

The Phone on my desk rang. I muted the sound on the TV as I watched Seamus O' Rourke bite Horst Gruber on the leg.

So much for celebrating diversity.

"Bear With Us Detective Agency, this is Bearstone. Can I help you?"

"Uh, yeah. The name's Kinsella. I've got a farm about five miles south of El Bruno and I'm having some trouble out here. Could you and your partner come out and take a look?"

"What sort of trouble?" I asked. "Must be pretty bad if you need both of us."

"Truth is, I don't know myself," he said. "The cops just come out and shake their heads at me. I don't think they even want to get out of the car anymore. Better if I show you."

We drove out to Kinsella's farm. It was one of those old-fashioned places where you drive up a long gravel driveway and are immediately surrounded by cornfields. The old farmhouse looked well kept.

Kinsella was a sandy-haired guy in his early thirties. He stepped off the porch and was smiling as he saw us get out of the car.

"Bearstone and the Wolf," he said. "I am so glad to see you two. I hope you can help."

We shook hands and he led us into the cornfield to the left of the house. We walked in about a hundred yards and stopped.

"I just want you to stand here and listen," Kinsella said. "It's a voice like a heavy whisper."

We stood for awhile. The breeze blew through the seven-foot tall corn.

"This gonna be like where the crop-duster tries to kill Cary Grant in North By Northwest?" Wolfie asked.

"No, no," Kinsella said. "It'll be like a whisper, a voice, maybe a prophet."

"Uh huh," Wolfie nodded.

And then it did seem like a voice had whispered.

"Hear that?" Kinsella asked. "If you build it, he'll come."

"Ain't what I heard," Wolfie said. "I heard the voice say your builder's a bum."

96

Kinsella looked at me.

"Well?"

"I thought it said, 'You got filth on your drum.'"

Kinsella shook his head.

"Wait awhile," he said. "The voice whispers other things. Really, it does. Look, here's five hundred bucks. Just stay awhile."

I looked at the Wolf. He shrugged.

"Okay, we'll stick around,"

It took awhile, but the whisper came again.

Kinsella smiled.

"Hear that, 'ease his pain'?"

"I heard 'Seas of Spain,'" Wolfie said.

Kinsella turned to me again.

"Please explain?" I shrugged.

We were all hearing different things.

"One more try, please?" Kinsella had his hands jammed into his pockets.

I nodded. The Wolf shrugged.

The voice came again.

"Hah. No doubt that time," Kinsella said. "Go the distance."

"Ain't what I heard," the Wolf said. "I heard goaty piss dance."

Kinsella turned to me again. His face was flushed red. He would have been a good fit for Harry Stringer's audience.

"No to Pistons," I said. "Don't bet Detroit in the NBA?"

"Maybe you bet 'em but take the points," the Wolf said.

"Look," I said. "We want to help, but standing here trying to figure out what the voice is saying might not be the right approach. Where do you think this voice is coming from?"

His face started to go pale. His mouth hung open.

"I uh just thought maybe it was some mystical being with some special message that would allow me to bring back people from the dead and square things up with them. You know, feel good stuff."

"You ain't talkin' about some chick flick, are you?" Wolfie asked.

We were standing in Kinsella's driveway.

"No, look around," he said. "I've got four thousand acres of corn. I plow, I plant, I wait, I harvest it and it all ends up in someone's gas tank as ethanol. It does absolute shit for engines. No one eats this crap. Hell, it's all GMO. How would you feel if this was your life? You'd be looking for some voice, too."

Just then we heard another voice. Only this time it seemed like it was louder and clearer as if someone had turned up the volume on p.a. system.

"Mr. White, are we done?"

"Have we filled the last drum?"

"We've filled the last drum."

"Jesse, it's plain.'

"We made a big gain."

"Well, Jesse let's go the distance."

The sound of a large engine approached. An RV burst out of the cornfield to our right and headed down the driveway for the open road.

"Uh, you running some kinda RV park?" Wolfie asked.

"There go your voices," I said. "Their all-weather speakers must have been on. When they started the engine, they got louder."

"Never knew they were there," Kinsella said. "I did smell some strange odors at odd hours."

"Bet they were cooking meth," I said.

"Think so?" Kinsella asked.

"They weren't making cough syrup," Wolfie said.

"I gotta do something else with this farm," Kinsella said. "A sports venue, maybe. Bowling. People love bowling, don't they? Think of the traditions, bowling shirts and beer frames. It's a big part of what's made America what it is today. I'll call it the Alley of Dreams."

"Then maybe you heard the voices right," I said. "If you build it, they'll come and bowl."

The Wolf grinned.

"And they can ease their pain at the Go the Distance Lounge."

The Tough Times Caper

I was hanging with my partner Wolfie in our office at the Bear With Us Detective Agency. We were eating jalapeno-flavored cannoli from the Hungry Bear Donut Factory and watching a recorded webinar put out by Neal (Before I Kill You) Carruthers of the Tough Guy Institute. The subject of the webinar was "Projecting Toughness."

The guy interviewing Neal looked like a turkey wearing a grey turtleneck sweater. His vocal range was somewhere up there with canaries. Not so Neal. His vocal range was more like the MGM lion trapped in an empty garbage truck.

"So, what are some of those things you can say to project toughness?" Tom Turkey asked.

"You want your adversaries to think you're in control and that you're the toughest thing they've ever dealt with," Neal said. "I've had guns pointed at me. So what? 'You might have enough guts to pull the trigger,' I tell them, 'But you're gonna die slow, and I'm gonna kill you.' They usually wet their pants about then."

"Wow, have you ever been shot?" Tom Turkey asked.

"Five times shot, four times married. A couple of the shootings were better than a couple of the marriages. In fact, a couple of the shootings were from the marriages. Every time, I came back tougher than I went in."

"You've been around a long time," Tom Turkey said. "Any advice for the aging tough guy?"

"Yeah. You got to know a few tricks. I throw a big party. I have a couple of friends meet me at the liquor store to help carry. Two barrels of beer and a case of booze. The trick is the barrel I carry is almost empty. I go skipping up two flights of stairs while my two friends struggle with their loads. They can't keep up with the old guy. At least, I let them think that.

"Another thing I do is describe things the proper way. Other guys might say that someone lost a lot of blood. Not me. I say, 'He Niagara-ed blood down the stairs into an ankle-deep pond.' You'll know you're doing it right when you get people fainting or people ready to toss lunch."

"You two loafing around again, watching this phony?" It was Beartina, bookkeeper, office manager and love of my life. "This is the same guy who cried like a baby when they sentenced him for tax evasion. He's doing three to five in a federal playpen."

I turned off the webinar.

"You boys need a webinar that tells you to get up off your butts and get to work." She said. "There's someone in the waiting area that needs your help. I'll send him in."

The familiar bearded face belonged to Nick Santos.

He shook hands with us and sat in the chair facing my desk. If anyone looked down and out, it was Nick.

"I decided to come back to town and take another crack at it," he said. "But, I have to tell you things don't look any better than when I left. In fact, they look worse."

I slid the tray of cannoli toward him.

"Careful, they have a bite," I said.

"Hey, maybe that's what I need," he said. "Something to shake me up. Get me going."

He took a bite and looked around the room.

"This year it's a Lexus, a red Lexus. Last year, it was a Mercedes, silver with a red ribbon on it, the year before that a BMW, light blue, if I remember right. Easy gig. Put on the suit, drive the luxury beast past the cameras so that people will want one. Yeah, everyone wants one, but who can afford one? Who really needs one? Oh, the fantasy that they'll find one under the Christmas tree in their fifteen room house they wished they owned, or out in the driveway where they're playing with their Labrador Retriever puppy in the snow that's been photo-shopped in."

"Yeah, it's what they call 'the spirit of the holiday'," Wolfie said. "It's one of those semi-religious events where everyone gets to save this whole mess from going down the tubes by buying stuff they don't need."

"Black Friday," Nick said. "Why don't they call it 'High Noon' or 'Armageddon?' Wouldn't that be more fitting?"

"Probably some copyright violation there," Wolfie said.

"Yeah," Nick said. "Everything's for sale. Pretty soon, somebody will own everything. Our very breaths will be metered and taxed."

"Only you're going to have to breathe extra during the holiday season so the whole thing doesn't collapse like a house of cards," Wolfie said. "They're going to have 'Inhalation Sunday' and 'Metabolic Monday.' I haven't figured out Tuesday, yet, but you can bet some money grubber is doing a study along with spreadsheets."

"Is there anything we can help you with?" I asked.

Nick fidgeted in his chair.

"You guys are good," he said. "Maybe you're the best. I want to hire you, but I don't have much money."

"Say that we work cheap," Wolfie said. "What can we do for you?"

102

"I want you to do nothing," Nick said. "When someone else hands you a ton of money to find me, I want you to say it's a conflict of interest. I'm already a client."

I looked at him. He smiled.

"Don't you worry, Bearstone. I'm not going to kill anyone."

"But you're going to disappear," I said.

"I'm already disappearing," he said. "I used to be a conduit for kids to explain what they wanted. Usually, there was something beautiful and shiny in the mix that damn near anyone could afford, a yo-yo, a small doll, a wind-up racecar. Now I'm a symbol of the one percent. Does Muffy want a new Mercedes so she won't be embarrassed when she meets her friends at the country club? Should Ralph have a new Lincoln so his boss won't think he's a loser?"

He crossed his legs, showing off his red pants and shiny black boots.

"Jesus, it's hot in here," he said. He unbuttoned his red jacket.

"Must be the jalapeno cannoli," Wolfie said.

"Maybe it's the fact that there's no snow from here to the North Pole," Nick said. "But we'll keep turning out limos for Muffy and Ralph. What the hell's a little global warming? Besides, children can't vote. They should be damn happy with what Ralph and Muffy decide to leave them."

I looked at him again. He was tired of it all. He had been a symbol of love and hope when you could buy a Coke for a dime or even a quarter. Now, he felt like a shill for people who could only express what remained of love with greed.

"Twenty bucks," I said. "If you've got it."

"Done," he said.

He got to his feet and slapped a twenty on the desk, shook our hands and left.

"Wow," said the Wolf. "There goes one pissed off Santa. Think anyone will care? I mean he ain't going to steal a car or nothing, is he?"

"I don't think so," I said. "Maybe he's just had enough. He's been so good in those commercials; maybe someone will come looking."

Time moved along. People began to notice that Santas were in short supply. In fact, there weren't any decent ones. A department store tried to hire Wolfie's scrawny nephew Chiseler to be a Santa, but that was a bad move. Chiseler wanted more than he gave to folks. He was caught pilfering a woman's purse while she leaned in to be in the photo of scrawny Santa and her two-year-old daughter.

Somehow, Nick Santos had created an exodus of Santas. Across the nation, no one decent wanted to play Santa. Anyone wearing a Santa suit was some kind of a bum.

Stores took notice of the missing Santa situation.

"The solution was right there in front of our faces," said Cyril Nightrider, manager of the Mega Mana Mall. "The beautiful Santa display with the elves and the Christmas trees was empty. It was just right for displaying Mercedes and Lincolns, and boy look at the bottom line. Free lollipops to snotty little kids cost money. But sell a few Mercedes, and you can bet my wife will be at the country club meeting her friends."

We did hear from Nick Santos. It was a postcard from one of the low-lying islands in the Pacific, threatened by rising seas.

"Our highest point on the island is 16 feet above sea level. Most of it's at the four-foot level. These people know what counts. We fish and surf and sing crazy songs. Seems like every week or so another guy who used to play Santa arrives. I'm happy to be here. Love to all, Nick."

The Lunatics Caper

It was early afternoon as my partner Wolfie and I entered the Bear With Us Detective Agency. We had each been on separate cases, working for the El Bruno Department of Mental Health.

I noticed that the desk where Beartina, our office manager, bookkeeper and receptionist usually sat was empty. Loud voices and the sound of a scuffle came from the inner office where Wolfie and I usually hung out.

"People lose teeth talkin' like that" a familiar voice said. "You wanna hang around, you'll be polite."

We barged through the doorway, ready for action.

Beartina sat in my swivel chair with her feet up on my desk. The TV was tuned to a Sam Spade movie, one of our favorite training films, filled with wise-guy patter. We were about to get a refresher course in snappy repartee, but suddenly the station switched to a commercial. The sounds of Steppenwolf's Magic Carpet Ride meant only one thing, Alladin Carpet and Lighting's long-winded spiel about decorating your home.

"Not this guy," Wolfie said. "His commercials go on for hours."

"Yeah, when we went to school with this guy wasn't his name something like Joe Murphy?" Beartina asked. "So how come he's Alladin, now? 'Cause he got a deal on a carload of fake oriental carpeting and magic genie lamps?"

"Hey, if you got a deal like that, you'd be calling yourself Scheherazade," Wolfie said.

"Maybe so," Beartina said. "I'd have better music than that useless Steppenwolf junk. I'd have that Rimsky-Korsakov suite, and I wouldn't go beating my gums as long as Joe 'Alladin' Murphy does."

I turned off the TV.

"We got work to do, cases to report on," I said.

"And I got banking and shopping to do," Beartina said. "I'm meeting your Mary, Wolfie. We're having lunch and going to our environmental investment club. I'm leaving the place to you two buzzards."

I watched as she wiggled her way out the door.

I sat down behind my desk and took out a tray of peppermint-favored cannoli from the Hungry Bear Donut Factory. The Wolf sat across the desk from me and opened his folder on the case he had been working.

"How bad was it?" I asked.

"Bad enough to have two cannoli," he reached for the tray.

Mental Health cases were like that. They were a mess to figure out and often had sad endings.

Wolfie crunched the end of a cannoli and opened his folder.

"Sad case, guy living alone with some kind of blackbird, maybe a crow flying around his apartment. We couldn't tell whether he was calling the bird 'Lenore' or something like 'Nevermore.' He claimed the bird talked to him, but we never heard anything more than a squawk."

I shook my head.

He continued.

"Wild bird in an apartment is against the house rules, but no cause for committing someone. Then this dude starts talking about how he chained someone up at a wine tasting and then bricked him up behind a wall to get

106

back at him; this happened someplace in Italy. He said he left the guy there to die. Interpol is checking on that one. But that ain't the end of it."

He took another bite of cannoli.

"He starts saying we should look under the floor. There's the heart of some dude he killed and it's still beating under the floorboards. He says it's the telltale heart. The only heart I can hear is some country band in the apartment below singing Your Cheatin' Heart."

"What happened then," I asked.

"He starts talking about this place where ushers hang out and where dead bodies started coming back to life and how the whole place cracked in half and fell apart and that was enough for the mental health guys. They gave him a quick injection and took him to the waiting ambulance. Eddie Poe is the guy's name. We have to send a bill and refer to his case for billing."

"Heavy stuff," I said.

"Yeah, but you caught the Gepetto case," Wolfie said. "That had to be rough."

"We knew this was coming," I said. "Him talking to a puppet like it was a kid. Then people thought he had a real kid living with him and they started wondering. Where'd this old coot come up with a kid? Did he grab the boy somewhere? He tells the school that he's sending the kid to class and when this kid doesn't show up, he makes a big excuse like some cat kidnapped the child and took him to a donkey farm."

"I remember all of that," Wolfie said. "Didn't he try to tell people that he did a Jonah and the whale act?"

"Yeah, he got swallowed by a whale named Monstro, but the kid came to his rescue. Somehow the whale sneezed and blew Gepetto out into the sea where he almost drowned. Then he claimed that the kid did drown but was brought back to life by the Blue Fairy. It gets worse. Gepetto contends that a cricket is now acting as the conscience of the kid."

"So, you got to his place and what happened?" Wolfie asked.

"Child Welfare was there with us. They wanted to see the kid. All Gepetto could do is point to a wooden marionette sitting on the counter. 'It's a Pinocchio,' he said. Child Welfare wouldn't buy it. Next thing you know, Immigration was there, too. They don't have a record of Gepetto entering the country. No green card, no passport. Who is this guy?"

"Wow," Wolfie said. "What happened then?"

"Gepetto tried to tell them he was born in New Jersey, but that fell on deaf ears. Homeland Security came and ran his prints. Next thing you know, there's an Amber alert out for this kid who may or may not exist. They don't even know what the kid looks like. When they asked Gepetto for a photo of the boy, he handed them a picture of the marionette."

"What about the neighbors? Any of them see the kid?"

"They saw Gepetto talking to the cricket and heard him talking to the kid and the Blue Fairy, but the closest thing to a kid that anyone saw was this marionette. They say the only thing the marionette could do was make his nose grow longer when Gepetto asked it questions."

"A ventriloquist's dummy," Wolfie said.

"And not a very good one at that," I said. "They took Gepetto away. He's somewhere in the federal system. They're digging up Gepetto's backyard to see what, if anything, is buried there. I was happy to get out of there. The agent in charge handed me some forms to fill out in triplicate to get paid."

"You sound like you don't want to do these mental health interventions anymore," Wolfie said.

"You tell me," I said. "They said that the next one available for us to work on was some guy who claimed to eat billy goats raw when they tried to cross his bridge. Lately, it seems his complaint has been that the billy goats have been lying to him and threatening him. Sound like anything you'd be interested in?"

Wolfie laughed and shook his head.

"Hey, maybe that Alladin's Carpet and Lighting commercial is over. Let's watch some more of Sam Spade."

"A capital idea, my good Wolf."

The Lost Loot Caper

"I should have worn a referee's shirt and brought one of those shiny whistles that hang around your neck," Wolfie said. "All these guys want to do is argue with each other."

We were waiting for the arrival of two at-each-others-throat clients at the Bear With Us Detective Agency.

It was mid-morning, and we had just finished comparing strawberry flavored cannoli to the lilikoi variety. To my mind, it was pretty much a draw.

"They're late," I said. "They're probably arguing about whether to take a cab, a bus, a limo, or walk."

"Yeah, and they say opposites attract," the Wolf said. "Attract trouble."

I nodded and looked at my watch

At one time the two opposites did attract.

Antgro, Inc, one of the country's largest agricultural companies had merged with Grasshopper Fun Industries. That had been five years ago. At first, it seemed like an odd merger. Antgro's management was straight-laced born-again, based in Keokuk, Iowa. The Antgro logo showed an ant wearing a straw hat, driving a tractor.

Grasshopper management was rumored to have had Mafia connections. Grasshopper was based in Vegas. Grasshopper's logo featured a grasshopper playing an electric guitar.

The merger went through, and for a while, profits surged.

Grasshopper managed to turn useless agricultural plots into profitable golf courses and ski resorts, but now there was some cash crisis that they thought Bearstone and the Wolf could solve. The two principals of the merged companies would arrive to spill their troubles out onto our well-worn carpet.

The intercom on my desk screamed to life as Beartina announced the arrival of our two clients.

"Elmer Hayrack and Dante Pitchfork are here for their appointment."

The two men walked in and sat in chairs fronting my desk.

"You guys know the Wolf," I said, pointing at our Naugahyde sofa. The Wolf nodded. Pitchfork and Hayrack nodded.

"Tell us your troubles," I said. "We want to help."

"We're missing 40 million bucks," Dante Pitchfork said. He wore a red suede jacket with a black shirt and a white tie.

"Hayrack here says someone got into our financials and hacked all our money. Right now we're both operating on credit."

"And airline miles," Hayrack said. "I also have a Costco Rewards coupon I haven't cashed yet."

Pitchfork rolled his eyes.

"Big time agro exec," he said. "Runs around in his Wal-Mart suit bragging about his Costco coupon. Jesus, Elmer. No shame, no class and no clue. We're out 40 mil, and you're acting like we're running a friggin' candy store."

Elmer Hayrack's face reddened.

"We'd be better off if we were," he said. "Before you showed up with your all-play-and–no-work business plan, Antgro had great profits. We grew corn to make ethanol. Got a nice government subsidy to do it, too. We also got paid for not growing tobacco. Keokuk people are firm believers in the American Way. We're not shiftless ghetto-dwellers living off food stamps."

"This American Way of yours must run right through a couple of nudie shows in Vegas," Pitchfork said. " 'The Empresses' New Clothes' ring a bell with you, Elmer? You were plenty happy when we counted the receipts from that one. Even happier when Sherry, one of the show gals, went hot-tubbing with you."

"Just a case of management and workers addressing each other's needs," Elmer said.

"Uh, you guys going back and forth isn't helping us," Wolfie said. "How about a little play-by-play on what happened to your 40 mil?"

"Yeah," I said. "You guys must have been doing something right to have 40 mil in the till. What happened?"

"I walked into my office one morning last week and turned on my computer," Elmer said. "A crazy looking Arab face cartoon pops up and says, 'The Forty Thieves have all your money. I can get it back for you. Signed Ollie Blah Blah, in El Bruno.' Some crazy sounds followed, and the screen went blank. I immediately got on another computer and got into our account at Too Big2Fail Bank. Our balance was $2008."

I had heard of Ollie Blah Blah. Rumor had it that he hung out in a dive in the Bottom Dollar Gulch section of town. The place was called Cy Burnett's.

I told Pitchfork and Hayrack that we'd take a look around and let them know what we found. They headed back to the Motel 6 after dropping a grand from their balance at Too Big2Fail Bank on our desk, with a promise of a much heftier reward if we found their dough.

We entered Cy Burnett's. It was a darkly lit bar with the usual trappings of a jukebox, loud drunks and bald bartender with apron tucked under his arms.

"Bearstone and the Wolf," the bartender said. "I think I know who you're looking for. He's in the last booth."

Ollie Blah Blah turned out to be a skinny kid just out of Stanford. He had other aliases, Ali Ba Ba, the Gingerbread Man, and John Dough, to name a few.

We sat across from him.

"I know why you're here," Ollie said. "But, I'm not sure I can help you very much. I'd like to. You know, we could share in any reward for bringing back the money, but I do not see any clear path here. I'm able to monitor big business' accounts by hacking in and seeing their activities. If I see something like this where 40 million is missing I try to trail the crooks, find the dough and collect the reward."

"So what's different about this one?" I asked.

"Their account never existed. It was all a dummy entry on their computer system that looked like a bank account, but never had any connection to a bank. It would be like if I wrote you a forty million dollar check on this bar coaster and if you went to cash it, they'd laugh in your face."

"So why would anyone do this?" The Wolf asked. "Where's the profit in that?"

"Good question," Ollie said. "Only works if you have a real account somewhere and you want to hide it all from say a partner."

"So, you say you're putting it all in a phony bank account, but you're putting it in another place where only you have access," I said. "Then you get someone to hack the phony account, and you're home free."

"Exactly," Ollie said. "You might even get someone to find some of the missing money, but it would all be a ruse to cover your trail."

"So, it could be Dante Pitchfork doing a number on shit kicking Elmer," Wolfie said.

"It's coming from the Antgro top dog," Ollie said.

"That's Hayrack," I said.

"Is he any relation to the Hayrack that's been running the 'I Beat Costco TV Sale' in vacant lots across from Costco, all over the country?"

"How's that work?" Wolfie asked.

"Word is he buys the TVs from Costco and somehow can sell them at half off. People are flocking to these sales. Cash only, but they go like hot cakes."

"So, how much are we talking about?" I asked.

"Thousands of TVs," Ollie said. "If he's really buying them from Costco on a credit card, just think how large his Costco Rewards Coupon would be for that."

We drove to the Motel 6.

Pitchfork answered the door.

"Come on in," he said. "Hayrack isn't here. He had a date with that tramp, Sherry. Is there a restaurant around here called Hong Kong Escape?"

114

The Crystal Ball Caper

The Wolf and I were sitting in our office at the Bear With Us Detective Agency. We were eating latkes, complete with applesauce, and sour cream that made you want to yell 'Mazeltov!' They were delivered hot from the Hungry Bear Donut Factory by Morrie Bearstein, one of the owners.

"You shouldn't eat too much," he warned us, "Or you won't have room for the blueberry blintzes."

It was good advice from Morrie, and the latkes were an excellent way to while away the time before our clients arrived. We were expecting the arrival of Rusty Flint and Earl E. Tinder, owners of Flint and Tinder Fire Insurance. They had something they wanted to share with us.

At ten, Beartina ushered the two men into our office. Flint sat in a chair in front of my desk. Tinder took a seat next to the Wolf on our Duncan Dempster Designed Naugahyde sofa.

"You boys called and said you had something bothering you," I said. "Care to let us know how we can help?"

Flint looked around the room and adjusted his tie as if he was about to do a Rodney Dangerfield impression.

"It's about our portfolio of clients," he said. "We like to know what's too risky and what might be a safe bet. We're not in this to lose our shirts."

"Stay with the roulette, then," Wolfie said. "House still has the advantage, but you can hang around the tables in Vegas for a long time sucking up their free drinks and making eyes at all the cuties."

Tinder burst out laughing and gave the Wolf a high five.

"I wish it were that easy," Flint said. "Thing is we sometimes have to take a forward look into what we're insuring. To give you an example, a lot of buggy whip manufacturers went up in flames shortly after Henry Ford brought out the Model T. The horseless carriage meant there was nothing left to whip. Their businesses went from cash cow to ash heaps. The 'accidental fires' were the only way out for some of them. More than a few insurance companies took a beating."

I nodded and looked at the Wolf.

He nodded.

We were good at nodding.

Flint adjusted his tie again.

"So we have to stay out in front of what might happen to some of the properties we insure," he said. "We have to be futurists."

"How are you going to do that?" Wolfie asked. "You got a crystal ball that maybe can tell you when the next Henry Ford is coming along?"

"We're looking into it," Tinder said from the couch.

"Yeah," Flint said. "You guys have heard of Charles Little, haven't you?"

"Yeah," I said. "Little's the guy on all the talk shows that has people opening envelopes that have his predictions inside. They're all sealed and have someone's signature and date on them, so there's no tampering. I've seen him."

"We have, too," Flint said. "We might be hiring him. He's been around for years. He predicted London

Bridge falling down, back when he was just getting started."

"I heard stories about that," I said. "Some think that Little had inside info on that developer wanting to reconstruct the bridge in Lake Havasu City. The city of London was doing its damnedest to get a replacement for the old bridge. What else has he done to impress you?"

"Back before no one ever heard of Tommy Tucker, the country star, Little predicted that Tucker would be singing for people's supper. Now Tucker's a big hit in supper clubs all over the country."

"Hasn't had a hit in awhile," the Wolf said. "He's got a nice voice, though."

"Well, Little had a big one come true when he said the Cubs would win the World Series," Flint said. "They showed him on ESPN opening the sealed envelope with his prediction inside."

"So, how can we help?" I asked. "Do you want us to investigate this guy?"

"Yeah, find out if he's for real," Tinder said.

They dropped three grand on my desk and made their way toward the door.

"We'll go see about this guy," I said.

The Little Institute was in Dire Straits, a town ten miles south of El Bruno. We pulled up to the address given us. It was a storefront office between a barber shop and a nail salon. A receptionist greeted us as we walked in.

I handed her my card and said we'd like to have a few minutes with Mr. Little.

"Do you have an appointment to see Ch... er, I mean Mr. Little?"

"Some clients of ours are interested in hiring him."

"Oh, well he just stepped out for a few minutes, so I'm trying to straighten out all the left over predictions we've accumulated. You're welcome to stay. He shouldn't be long."

Her name was Inez.

She got up from her desk and grabbed an empty cardboard box from a stack near the door leading to a back room.

"I've got a lot of old predictions to toss out," Inez said and disappeared into the back room.

"Whole bunch of envelopes in that box over there," Wolfie said. "All sealed and signed over the opening with dates on them.

I looked. The lettering on the box said "2016 World Series Predictions."

"Slide that over here," I said.

I opened the first envelope marked "Indians."

"The Cleveland Indians will be World Series champs in 2016," was written on the paper inside.

I opened another.

"The Boston Red Sox will be World Series champs in 2016."

The Wolf opened one.

"Giants," he said.

I opened one.

"Cardinals."

Every Major League team was in an envelope. All Little had to do to impress the public was produce the right envelope after the Series winner was determined. Doing it on ESPN impressed a lot of people, including our clients, Flint and Tinder.

I noticed other boxes of envelopes around the office. One said "Apple Stock Forecast." Another said, "Super Bowl Teams Forecast."

Inez came back to the front with another box of envelopes.

"More World Series predictions?" Wolfie asked.

"No, these are the predictions for the presidential race," Inez said. "You can see in each corner of the envelope a penciled number and a letter. This one says 316 C. That would mean 316 electoral votes for Clinton. She didn't get that, so we toss this away. Mr. Little took his prediction envelope to Fox News this time to open it with his exact correct prediction of Mr. Trump's win. They were very impressed."

A well-cared for DeLorean pulled up to the curb outside. A magnetic sign on its door read, "Profit From the Future, Little Institute, Dire Straits."

"Oh, that's Chick now," Inez said.

"Chick?" I asked. "I thought his name was Charles or Chuck."

"He changed it from Chick to Charles," Inez said. "He had that one bad prediction when he started out. Claimed there would be a disastrous snowfall in Hawaii, of all places. The media gave him a great working over when it didn't happen."

She reached into her desk for a file and opened it. It held copies of newspaper headlines: 'Chick N. Little Yells Sky Falling, Nothing Happens!' and 'Chick N. Little in Fowl Mood When Sky Doesn't Fall.'

I grabbed a plain envelope off Inez's desk and wrote 'Brooklyn Dodgers' on it. I put a message on the back of one of my cards, slid it into the envelope and sealed it.

We headed for the front door.

Little met us on the sidewalk.

"Gentlemen, anything I can do for you?" Little asked.

I handed him the envelope.

"One of our predictions, Chick."

We got into our car and drove away.

"What'd you write on that card you put in the Brooklyn Dodger envelope?" The Wolf asked.

"I wrote, 'Congratulations, Chick. If your DeLorean can make it back to 1955, you can come to work for Flint and Tinder.' That's the only time the Brooklyn Dodgers won the World Series."

The Literary Caper

The El Bruno International Amphitheatre was filling up with participants in the First Annual El Bruno Literary Fest. My Partner Wolfie and his wife Mary were steadying a ladder holding the love of my life Beartina. She was hanging a large banner over my booth. It was supposed to have read, "Hard-Boiled Detective Tells it Like it is!"

Unfortunately, letting Wolfie's nephew Shyster make a deal for the sign resulted in, "Half-Baked Detective Spills the Beans!"

"Don't matter what it says," Beartina said from atop the ladder. "People are gonna love your book of stories."

Okay.

The book was an accident of sorts.

Sonny Duke and his lady Samantha Greywitch were headed to the Big Apple to promote her new cookbook, Cooking With Friends. A controversy was brewing over the book. A teenaged girl named Gretel had accused Samantha of cannibalism. The only way to fight the accusations was to do the book tour, getting on *Ellen* and whoever else would have Samantha as a guest. The fact that Sonny had more money than a particular reality show-based politician didn't hurt.

Sonny had visited my office before they boarded their flight.

"We could use your case notes on the Samantha and Gretel controversy," he said. "In fact, I wouldn't mind reading any of the cases you'd like to share. You've got some interesting stories."

Beartina made some copies of some cases and handed them to Sonny.

Two weeks later, I got a call from someone named Cornell Milquetoast III, editor of The New Hawker Magazine. Sonny Duke and Samantha Greywitch had dropped by his office.

"I'm fascinated by some of your stories," he said. "We'd like to publish some of them. They're an incredible rendering of fiction in a Twain or Vonnegut tradition."

I could have said, "Hey Cornell, they're not fiction. You can't make shit up like this," but I let him ramble on until he got to the essence of publishing.

"We'd like to give you $1500 for each story, upon publication. The rights to the stories will revert to you so you could make a book out of them. In fact, we could make a deal to publish the book ourselves and push it pretty hard with our magazine."

While Cornell Milquetoast III rambled on, I got on his website and discovered that he was indeed in charge of The New Hawker Magazine publishing empire. He had succeeded his father and his grandfather in the business.

On the website were pictures of various Milquetoasts with famous writers. The original Milquetoast stood next to Ernest Hemingway, aboard PILAR in Havana Harbor. Hemingway wore a rugged fisherman's sweater; Milquetoast wore what looked like a tuxedo. Both had a wide smile as if they had both landed a prize fish. The more I thought about it, the more it seemed fitting. Milquetoast would hang the picture in his New York office to show his cronies that he had landed a Hemingway. Hemingway would hang his copy of the photo in some place like the Floridita Bar to show his pals that he had landed another publisher willing to pay for the next round of drinks and then some.

The pattern of tuxedo-clad Milquetoasts and well-known writers in photos continued.

Cornell Milquetoast II sat in his tux next to Alan Ginsburg and Jack Kerouac in a North Beach bar with Lawrence Ferlinghetti looking on.

Cornell Milquetoast III in tuxedo sat next to Kurt Vonnegut who wore a blue work shirt and a puzzled look. If you could read minds, Vonnegut was probably wondering why this guy wore a tux.

I scanned the crowd to see if anyone dressed in a tuxedo was headed my way.

Not yet.

I wanted a photo of Milquetoast III and me in front of our booth.

My 200 books looked great on the table.

Bearstone Blackie, Detective.

I looked to my right. The display next to me had books by a woman who had discovered a secret code used by the Zoroastrians. Her book, Stars and Your Future claimed that both Ronald Reagan and Elvis were emissaries from the Vortex.

To my left was another bookseller, a survivalist who advocated living in the tunnels beneath Las Vegas. His book was Subterranean Go for Broke.

Across from me stood another display, Decorating with Shotgun and Machete.

There was certainly a variety of books on display.

I noticed that several of the booths had large crowds in front of them. I walked over.

The large sign above one booth said, "Creative Licenses."

A fat man wearing a top hat and a red vest stood behind the table.

"Cuthbert T. Willy at your service," he said. "You look like a creative type. You a writer? A poet?"

I nodded.

"A writer."

"Literary license, five bucks. Do any poetry?"

"Sometimes."

"Painting, sculpture?"

"A cartoon or two."

"Well, here's what you need," the fat man said. "The Deluxe Creative License Package gives you poetic license, literary license, and artistic license. All in one, ten bucks, and you can take it off your income tax."

I told him I'd think about it and walked on to where the next crowd had gathered.

The sign above the table read, "Churchill Shakespeare Literary Conceit Enter Now."

At the table, people were filling out forms and paying fifteen dollars to enter.

A man dressed in tweeds spoke with an English accent.

"Jolly well, now. We're into our three-hundredth year of the Conceit, and we've gloried in such winners as Tennessee Wilson, William Falconer, and J.K. Growling. Enter your best effort now. You could be the next big thing in literature."

It was a two-part form. You took your receipt with you. It told you how to load your story or poetry into the Conceit's submission folder. It seemed the line in front of their booth had grown to several hundred waiting to register.

As I looked at the line, I noticed that back at my booth stood a man wearing a tuxedo. It had come. My Milquetoast moment was here.

I rushed back.

"Bearstone," Cornell Milquetoast III said. "Can we make a photo together? I'd hang it in my office, and we can use it for publicity."

"I'd like that," I said. "I'll need a few copies for my office and other places." I didn't know how he'd feel about his photo hanging in the Hungry Bear Donut Factory or the Ribs and Peppers Bistro.

We took some photos, and people started to gather in front of my books.

Could I autograph them?

Certainly.

Would they like a sack for the book?

Of course, Hungry Bear Donut Factory sacks.

Could I autograph them?

Certainly.

The books began to sell and soon we were down to only a few remaining. I walked over to our neighbors and gave them each a book.

They were happy to get them. I bought a book from each neighbor.

You never knew when you'd need to know about the Zoroastrian Vortex, or how to live under the streets of Vegas. Even decorating with a shotgun and a machete had its possibilities.

We went to dinner with Wolfie and Mary. It felt great to be with good friends and be a successful author.

Later, I kept thinking about the Churchill Shakespeare Literary Conceit and the guy in tweeds who spoke in the jolly Brit accent.

His face was familiar.

I had seen him before, selling "Rolex" watches for forty bucks apiece at the El Bruno Flea Market.

This literary racket was a tough business.

The Reality Caper

Roshi Kensho, our visiting Zen instructor at the Bear With Us Detective Agency, was about to leave my partner Wolfie and me with a couple of koans that we were to contemplate. Roshi thought it would make us better detectives if we could intuitively understand a situation, rather than waste time asking about who, what, where and when.

"A real Zen detective needs to make his mind blank while he contemplates the folly of reality," Roshi said, grabbing the last mint-flavored cannoli.

"Koan number one," he said. "If tin whistles are made of tin, from what do they make fog horns?"

The Wolf looked at me.

I looked at Roshi.

"You are not to waste your energy thinking about this with a full mind," he said. "Your intuitive mind will lead you to where you are meant to go."

I nodded.

The Wolf nodded.

"Your second koan," he said. "Time flies like an arrow, but fruit flies like a banana."

I looked at the Wolf.

He stared back at me.

"No need to start your meditation while I am here," Roshi said. "Remember, there are many variations of reality, just as there are many variations of cannoli."

He got to his feet and bowed deeply to both of us and left the office.

Beartina wiggled her way in.

"Bearstone, I heard what that Roshi guy said about reality," she said. "My version of reality is I have to go do the banking and the shopping. I'll leave you two birds here to meditate. Maybe do you some good."

She was out the door.

I looked at the Wolf. He was already meditating so well that he had a gentle snore going. Lucky for him to be stretched out on our Duncan Dempster designed Naugahyde sofa.

I leaned back in my chair and stared at the ceiling fan as it slowly turned above my head.

Several minutes into my meditation, I noticed that somehow the television was on in the office.

"An exciting day here on the Mississippi River," the announcer said. "We're getting into the finals of the Airbus A320 Extravaganza. We're delighted to be here with one of the founders of this sport, Will Getz, founder of Kumquat Computers. Mr. Getz, give us a brief rundown as to how the Airbus A320 Extravaganza got started."

"Hey Tony, just call me Will," Getz said. "I may be a billionaire, but I put on my $2,000 Brooks Brothers Alligator loafers just like any working stiff, one foot at a time."

"Uh, okay Will, uh tell us about how the A320 got started."

"Yeah goes back to the drama on the Hudson when Captain Sully Sullenberger landed his Airbus A320 on the Hudson after hitting a flock of birds. Everyone saw the plane floating in the river afterward and all the people getting off safely. A hundred and fifty-five people evacuated in minutes, a tremendous feat. Many people wanted to know more about the landing. Millions wished they could have seen it happen. I was one of them. I called a few friends. They felt the same way."

"And was one of the friends Vegas billionaire Addley Shellington?" Tony asked.

"Yeah, he started us down the road when he said, 'you don't think this Sully guy is the only one who can land an Airbus on water, do you?' I told him no. I bet him there were hundreds of guys who could do that."

"Is that when he said, 'And there are millions of people who would pay to see that happen'?"

"Yes, Tony. That's how the National Flotation League was started. From humble beginnings on the Hudson, we now have teams from around the country competing in the Airbus A320 Extravaganza. Who can make that perfect landing? Unload their 155 people on board and make it safely to the shore in record time? We estimate two billion viewers will be witnessing today's competition on pay television."

"Not everything goes right in Airbus competition," Tony said. "I think you know where I'm headed?"

"Oh yeah, the semifinals in Lake Tahoe," Will said. "It was terrible that all those people on the Texas entry lost their lives, but our pilots tell us that videos of that incident are helping pilots all over the world to fly better and safer. Over twelve million pilots have ordered the videos of that incident on Blu-Ray. That's a lot of pilots. It's our way to promote safety in the air."

"And a lot of hooey, if you ask me."

I looked up. It was Grizz Lee Bearloft, the inventor of the FlashDark and other items he had the Wolf and me testing.

"Sit down, Grizz," I said. "Be careful not to wake the Wolf, he's busy meditating. Our Zen instructor was in here a little while ago instructing us about the different versions of reality."

"You mean like that crap on television?" He pointed at the screen now showing a fireball in slow motion coming from a large body of water. The announcer was saying something about ordering the Tahoe Videos now and getting free shipping. The price $79.99 flashed on the screen.

I turned down the sound.

"Reality shows," Grizz scoffed. "People tune into them. They're like professional wrestling, all show, not much reality. The powers-that-be make it hard to tell the difference between real reality and fake reality."

"Care to expound on that?" I asked.

"We had a B-movie actor who became the governor and then went on to be president," Grizz said. "Then we had an actor who became the governor who now is hosting a reality show formerly run by a reality show guy who moves into the White House to run the whole show. Does anyone care who gets fired on the Celebrity Intern Show? No, people just tune in to see somebody get fired. It's like pro football. They should call that Celebrity Concussion Protocol. If they hired Matt Damon to announce the games, they could call it The Bourne Concussion Protocol."

Grizz was wound up, but it didn't disturb the Wolf. He was deep into meditation, punctuating each insight with a snuffle snore.

"So, what's the answer to a nation that has trouble separating reality from reality shows?" I asked. "Is Kylie Jenner going to be nominated to be on the Supreme Court?"

Grizz leaned back in his chair and grinned.

"I've been working on this problem," he said. "I have a prototype that could be the answer to all this confusion. I'm calling it the Kardashian Filter."

"The Kardashian Filter?"

"Works with others, not just her, but she's one of the worse. Ten million people are following this airhead around, thinking they're getting real insight into her life. What's she going to do with Kanye or Caitlyn Jenner? Why should anyone care? Why should anyone with a brain have to be assaulted by headlines on Google News worrying about the latest garbage from this woman?"

He took a small black box out of his valise and pressed a button on the top. A voice responded.

"I'm Iris, how can I serve you?"

"Iris, in thirty seconds, replace the Airbus Extravaganza with a video of people surfing to Hawaiian music."

I turned up the sound on the television. Flames were shooting out of a wrecked airplane.

"That's right, Tony," Will Getz said from the screen. "A terrible crash in the first heat a few minutes ago. We have a drone cam hovering over the flaming wreckage."

Then the picture changed to sunny Waimea Bay on Oahu. Brother Iz was singing about rainbows. People were surfing and laughing.

I looked up into the whirling ceiling fan.

"Wonderful invention," I said.

"Ceiling fans sure are," Beartina said. She was back from her errands.

"You been meditating or just sleeping like the Wolf?"

I looked around. Grizz was gone. The Black box was gone. The TV was off.

"I guess I was dreaming," I said, "But I got some insights into the reality question."

"Anything you want to share, Sugar?" She smiled at me.

"Of all my different realities, you're the best."

"Oh," she said. "You're just looking for a big kiss."

"Maybe two, if you're not in a hurry," I said.

About the Author

Ray Pace lives in Waikoloa Village on the Big Island of Hawaii. He is frequently found at writer gatherings in Waimea, Hawi, and Kona. Reach him at raypacewrites@gmail.com.

His website is www.raypaceatlarge.com.

He is also the author of *Hemingway, Memories of Les*, a book about his friendship with Leicester Hemingway, author of *My Brother, Ernest Hemingway*.

Soon to be published:

Hemingway's Hawaii Letter, a WWII adventure.

Disappearing Act, an action detective story that takes place in Las Vegas.

Made in the USA
Columbia, SC
30 December 2021